VINTAGE

A GLIMPSE OF MY LIFE

Ram Prasad 'Bismil' (1897–1927) was an Indian revolutionary who dedicated his life to the cause of India's liberation from British rule. He was a central figure in the now-famous Kakori train dacoity, an attempt to raise funds for the revolutionary movement against British control. After he was arrested, he was condemned to death and executed. He penned his autobiography while he was on death row, completing it on 16 December, just days before he was hanged on 19 December 1927.

Awadhesh Tripathi is a translator and literary critic based in Bhopal. He has translated several books into Hindi, including Ganesh Devy's *After Amnesia,* Gyanesh Kudasya's *India in the 1950s* and Richard Eaton's *India in the Persianate Age.* His monograph *Kavita Ka Loktantra* is a study of post-Independence Hindi poetry and its critique of the newly established Indian democracy.

OTHER BOOKS IN THE CHRONICLES SERIES

Courtesy of Criticism: Selected Essays of Kirtinath Kurtkoti (edited and translated from the Kannada by Kamalakar Bhat)

My Truth: Autobiography of Narmadashankar Dave (translated from the Gujarati by Abhijit Kothari)

A Glimpse of My Life

Autobiography of an Indian Revolutionary
Ram Prasad 'Bismil'

Translated from the Hindi by
Awadhesh Tripathi

VINTAGE
An imprint of Penguin Random House

VINTAGE

Vintage is an imprint of the Penguin Random House group of companies
whose addresses can be found at global.penguinrandomhouse.com

Published by Penguin Random House India Pvt. Ltd
4th Floor, Capital Tower 1, MG Road,
Gurugram 122 002, Haryana, India

| Penguin
Random House
India

First published in Vintage by Penguin Random House India 2025

Translation copyright © Awadhesh Tripathi 2025

ISBN 9780143467021

Typeset in Adobe Caslon Pro by MAP Systems, Bengaluru, India
Printed at Replika Press Pvt. Ltd, India

www.penguin.co.in

MIX
Paper | Supporting
responsible forestry
FSC™ C016779

About the Chronicles Series

The Ashoka Centre for Translation, through its initiatives, is committed to thinking about translation from a many-to-many perspective to foster India's multilingual ethos. Chronicles is a groundbreaking non-fiction translation series aimed at bringing creative–critical textual narratives from various Indian languages into English. In the inaugural list supported by the Manju Deshbandhu Gupta Fellowship, ten books are being published in partnership with Penguin Random House India.

translation.ashoka.edu.in

Contents

Translator's Note   ix

1. Self-Portrait   1
2. Love for the Country   51
3. On My Own   81
4. An Expanded Organization   101

Translator's Note

Ram Prasad 'Bismil' was one of the founders of the Hindustan Republican Association, a revolutionary organization with the aim of freeing India from British rule. Bismil is remembered in the history of India's freedom movement for his involvement in the Kakori case—a daring train robbery carried out by him and his revolutionary comrades on 9 August 1925 near Kakori railway station in what is now Uttar Pradesh. Bismil and his comrades stopped the train between two stations and took away the money being transported on it—an audacious challenge to the British government. He and his comrades (notably, Ashfaqullah Khan and Roshan Singh) were caught, put on trial and subsequently hanged on 19 December 1927.

This autobiography is the story of a revolutionary who lived and died with the single aim of freeing his motherland from foreign rule. In *Nij Jiwan Ki Ek Chhata*, Bismil reflects on his life, his family, the people and ideas that influenced and inspired him, and the revolutionary movement he built. He considers his mother and his guru to be his greatest teachers, and he writes of them as people who shaped his character, and gave him the strength and courage to choose the path he did in his life. Bismil tells us of his Arya Samaji roots, the books he reads and translates, his entry into revolutionary activities, the Mainpuri episode and the famous Kakori case.

He, like other revolutionaries of that time, was highly inspired by the Russian Revolution of 1917 and studied it to understand the requirements of the Indian context better. In his autobiography, he writes about how to work towards the social, political and economic freedom of the country. He is eventually convinced that the revolutionary struggle must be a mass movement, where weapons, as tools of anti-colonial struggle, must be used alongside literature and other popular forms for mass mobilization. Bismil reflects on class divisions in Indian society, being well aware that the class interests of the rich lie with the government, and he therefore stresses upon the need to unite the working classes under the banner of communism.

Bismil recognizes the limitations of revolutionary work in India; he rues the lack of experience or a clear strategy for taking down the Empire, the severe financial difficulties, a hostile regime and a lack of popular support, leading to mistakes in the work of the organization. Even as prisoners, the revolutionaries failed to put up a united strategy for promoting their cause or negotiating with the government, and ended up pursuing their individual cases, even leading to treachery and betrayal by fellow activists. He speaks of this with bitterness. Yet, he does not consider his work a waste. He is very much aware that his legacy will take the struggle for India's freedom to another level. Till his last breath, he championed the cause of unity between Hindus and Muslims. Again and again, he gives the example of his friendship with Ashfaq, which withstood not only religious differences but also political repression, as an example for all Indians to reject communal divisions.

Nij Jeevan Ki Ek Chhata is a valuable text both for its historical and literary value. Bismil's narration of his own story is interspersed with poetry. Some of the couplets are his own compositions, and he also quotes a few lines from the Gita and from Kabir. Interestingly, Bismil's prose is in Khadi Boli, while his couplets are in the tradition of Braj and Urdu poetry. In the Hindi literary sphere of the 1910s and the following decades, Mahavir Prasad Dwivedi, the editor of *Saraswati* magazine, initiated a debate regarding the choice of language and its use in different formats of writing. Till then, Khadi Boli was not considered a suitable language for poetry; poems were composed in Braj or Urdu. Dwivedi argued that the language of prose and poetry should be the same. A reading of Bismil's text reveals that he was influenced by the earlier tradition.

Despite its uneven narrative quality, this is a passionate account which moves the reader with its sincerity. Bismil comes across as a proud, self-aware and extremely considerate person who did not hesitate to put others' interest before his own well-being. At the individual level, he is proud of his self-discipline and his strength in staying true to the ideals. But even at a deeper level, he is justifiably proud of his contributions to the revolutionary movement he built, the responsibilities he shouldered, his loyalty to his comrades and his ultimate sacrifice in the service of the nation. The readers will find themselves inspired by the revolutionary fervour and deeply saddened by the fate of the martyrs.

Bismil wrote his autobiography in secret while he was in jail, on death row. He penned it on loose sheets of paper, which were smuggled out of the prison in three parts with the help of a sympathetic warder. He completed it just two days before his death. It first reached Dashrath Prasad Dwivedi, a journalist in Gorakhpur, who then shared it with Ganesh Shankar Vidyarthi, the editor of *Pratap*, a nationalist newspaper published from Kanpur. Vidyarthi published Bismil's story in 1928 as *Kakori Ke Shaheed* (The Martyrs of Kakori). This text was seized by the British government. However, the government did create an English summary of Bismil's story for their own knowledge of its contents, and this was made part of its confidential records. This English summary is now kept at the Criminal Investigation Department office in Lucknow.

Readers will no doubt find many of Bismil's ideas—about freedom and nation-building—and his stand against inequality and communalism to be still relevant to the Indian context. I hope that this English translation will encourage them to re-engage with Bismil's vision and his commitment to the nation.

August 2024   Awadhesh Tripathi
Bhopal

1

Self-Portrait

Kya hi lazzat hai ki rag-rag se aati hai sada
Dam na le talwar jab tak jaan Bismil mein rahe.

(Every vein in the body joyously declares
Bismil's sword shall not rest as long as he breathes.)

Two villages of Tomarghat, along the banks of the Chambal River, are especially famous in the kingdom/state of Gwalior, for the villagers here are notoriously defiant of the authorities. So much so that the zamindars here pay the land revenue as and when it pleases them, and in some years, they may not pay any at all. If a tehsildar or an administrative officer comes to claim the revenue, the inhabitants of these villages simply hide in the region's ravines and may stay put there for months. Their household, cattle and food move with them into the ravines. They are smart enough to not leave any valuable items back in their homes, which the state may auction off to extract revenue. A story that is often told here is that of a zamindar who in fact got a piece of land in pardon, despite not paying the revenue on it for years. He managed to hoodwink the officials for years before he was arrested and tortured. He was tied and left without food or water for days and finally threatened with being burnt alive—a small haystack was kept near his feet and set on fire. It is said that the zamindar remained unperturbed, sardonically remarking that the treasury of the maharaja (of Gwalior) would not run into losses if the zamindar did not pay up. And the world would remember this individual for his audacity and fearlessness. The officials informed the Gwalior court, which thought it wiser to not only let the zamindar go but also awarded him the land rent-free in perpetuity. Yet another story is of the villagers stealing sixty camels from the maharaja's cavalry unit and hiding them in the ravines. The maharaja ordered that both the villages be blasted to smithereens by cannon fire. It must have taken very difficult negotiations, on the one hand, to persuade the villagers to return the animals, and on the other, to cajole the maharaja into going back on his decision and not destroy the villages of these very stubborn yet brave people. Now, the villagers do not bother the locals so much; instead, they frequently raid the British territories and steal from the houses of the rich and return into hiding in the ravines. Once in the ravines, it is impossible for any police or army to find them, let alone punish them. Both these villages are on the banks of the Chambal, about 15 miles from the British territory. My grandfather (Dada-ji), Narayanlal-ji, was born here, into one of the illustrious families of the region. He left his paternal home because of bitterness among the family members and his sister in-law's hostile behaviour. He wandered in the area with his wife and his two sons and finally settled in Shahjahanpur. My father, Muralidhar-ji, was his eldest, and only eight years old then. My uncle (*chacha*, Sri Kalyanmal) was his younger son and six years old. This was the time of a brutal famine.

Difficult Days

After a long search, Sri Narayanlal-ji found a job at 3 rupees a month with one Mister Attar. How was a family of four to sustain themselves in a famine with a measly sum of 3 rupees? My grandmother (Dadi-ji) tried to sustain the children by eating only half a meal, once a day, but even this was hardly enough. She tried to keep her family from going hungry by using grains like bajra, kukni, sanwa, jowar, and on worse days, half a portion of the cheapest grain mixed with half a portion of the cheapest saag available, with some salt, was the only meal for Dadi-ji and Dada-ji. The sons were given chana or jau rotis. Half-hungry always, they would somehow live through the day, but the nights were especially difficult on an empty stomach. It was impossible for the family to get basic minimum food. How were they to manage clothes and a place to live? Dadi-ji tried to get small, petty jobs at the families of respectable people in the neighbourhood. But who would be willing to put their trust in a woman whose antecedents were unknown and who didn't speak like she was a local? No one would employ her or even give her grains to grind into flour, for they feared that she might eat the grains herself; those were the days of the famine, after all. It was only after many attempts of persuasion and requests for work that one or two women decided to give Dadi-ji some grains to make flour, but this upset the other women who had been previously hired for this work. There were many obstacles in finding work. If she found a job, it was barely to grind five–seven *ser* of grains and the wage was 1 paise per *panseri* (5 sers). It was three to four hours of hard labour to get 1 or 1.5 paise, and then she would return home to prepare food for the family. This was how two to three years were spent. Dada-ji would often wonder if they should return to their parental home, but Dadi-ji was firm that it was better to die here than return to a life of humiliation. She always felt that they had left their homeland, property, money, but it was impossible to bow in servitude to the people because of whom they were in this situation; they were witnessing bad days, but this too would pass. She faced terribly difficult times but did not once think of returning.

It was after about five or six years, when Dadi-ji became a familiar face, that the local women began to trust her and sympathize with her. They could see that she was from a good, decent family which had fallen on bad times. And the famine had ended.

She would now, once in a while, get some food in charity from the families living nearby, or a meal from a Brahmin home. Some days were spent thus. A few childless families approached and tried to cajole Dadi-ji into giving away one of her sons in exchange for money. But Dadi-ji was an ideal mother; she did not care for any riches and continued to raise her children as best she could in the circumstances.

The family managed some savings after years of labour and a little bit of work as *purohit*s, and this money was used to send my father to school. Dada-ji also started earning a slightly better salary of 7 rupees a month. In some time, he left his job to work as a money-changer, dealing with *duaani*, *chavvani*, etc. Things got better and the family starting seeing a daily income of 5–7 annas. Courage and hard work had borne the family out of hard times, and the credit for this goes to the revered Dadi-ji. Her patience and fortitude surely appeared to be divinely inspired, beyond human capacity. How else would an illiterate woman from a village work, earn a wage to feed and educate her children in extremely distressing circumstances—a woman who had never stepped out of her home, who had spent her life in a strict and orthodox Hindu environment where its followers were willing to die in defence of their traditions and customs; where a woman of a Brahmin, Kshatriya or Vaishya family would not dare to step out or visit another's home without a *ghunghat*.

Even the Shudra women could not be out of their homes without veiling their faces. The clothes worn by the Shudras were anyway different from those worn by the other castes, so that they could be instantly recognized, even from a distance. And these customs have taken the form of oppression. There was this instance of a Chamar bride who had returned to the village upon her wedding in the British territory. As was the custom, she went to the zamindar's house to pay her respects. Her attire was that of a Shudra woman but she wore *bichhiya* (toe ring) on her feet. The zamindar noticed her toe rings and asked of her caste. On being told that she was Chamar, he went inside his home and again came out wearing shoes. He came close to the Chamar woman, stepped on her toes, putting all his weight on her feet. Her toes were badly cut. He commented that if Chamar women now dared to wear toe rings, what would upper-caste women wear? The people here were uneducated and foolish, yet steeped in caste pride. No matter how educated or rich or elderly a Shudra might be, he would have to bow (*pailaagan*, *juhar*) before even the most uneducated or the poorest or even the young ones of the upper castes. If he failed to do so, he would be beaten with shoes, and it would be his own fault. If a daughter-in-law or daughter was suspected of adultery, she would, without a single thought, be killed and dumped in the Chambal. If a widow was found to be an adulteress or of 'loose morals', she too would be dismembered and thrown in the river, even if she was carrying a child. People would be none the wiser about the fate of the woman. These people were men of honour and values who would not hesitate to give up their lives to protect the honour of their women. It was Dadi-ji who alone could have the courage to do all that she did while being a married woman, maintaining all the customs of her land.

The difficult days finally came to an end, by God's grace. Pita-ji managed to get some education and Dada-ji bought a house. The family which had once trudged from door to door had a place to settle down, and it was now time to think of my father's marriage. Dadi-ji travelled to her maternal home with Dada-ji and Pita-ji, where my father was married off. They stayed there for a few months and then returned home with the bride.

Life at Home

After marriage, Pita-ji found a job in the municipality at a monthly wage of 15 rupees. He did not like this job very much and neither did he have much education. He stayed put in this job for a couple of years and then left it to start his own independent work of selling government stamps at the local court. Most of his life was spent at this work, and through it, he managed to sustain his family, educate his children and become a respectable member of his locality. As side businesses, he loaned money on interest and also owned three bullock carts which were given on hire. Pita-ji loved to exercise. He would regularly wrestle at the *akhada*, and his body was firm and strong.

His first child was a boy, who died. A year later, your author (Sri Ram Prasad) was born in the Shukla Paksha 11 of Vikrami Samvat 1954. Dada-ji desperately tried to protect my fragile body through the power of amulets, vows and talismans. Still, even two months after my birth, I was very weak and nearly in the condition of the first child who had died. Someone advised the family to catch a white rabbit, circle it around my body and release it on the ground. If there was an ailment, the rabbit would take it and die. And that was what happened. The rabbit managed only three or four rounds on the floor before it collapsed. I believe that this may be possible, because remedies (*aushadhi*) are of three kinds: divine, human and demonic. Demonic remedies take the character of birds' or animals' flesh and blood, and their use is mentioned in medicinal literature. One of the most intriguing and astonishing ways these have been employed is the case of using a bat for treating rickets in very young children. A child who is only a month or two old can recover from rickets by sucking the blood of a bat. This is a proven and effective remedy shared by a much-respected mahatma.

I was seven years old when Pita-ji himself taught me the Hindi alphabet and put me in a *maktab* under a maulvi sahib's tutelage to learn Urdu. I vividly remember the days when Pita-ji would regularly practise at the *akhada* and easily wrestle with and defeat young men who were nearly one and a half times his size. Pita-ji also became good friends with Sri Chatterjee, a Bengali man who ran a shop of allopathic medicines (*angrezi dawai*). Sri Chatterjee was also heavily addicted to *charas* and would always be at his *chillum*. Pita-ji picked up the addiction in his company and his body was soon wasted. At ten, I could see his bones sticking out of his body. Mister Chatterjee began drinking alcohol too, which irreparably damaged his liver. He died. Pita-ji agreed to give up marijuana after my vehement and stubborn protests, but did so very slowly only after many days.

There were five sisters and three brothers after me. Dadi-ji insisted that the girls born in the family should be killed at birth, as per custom, but my Mata-ji protested against this and saved the girls' lives. This was the first instance in our family lineage when girls were nurtured. Out of these siblings, two girls and two boys died. Now (in the year 1927 AD), I have one ten-year-old brother and three sisters. My sisters were educated and then married off in style, all because of Mata-ji's efforts. Never before had girls been married from the family; none had been allowed to live.

Dada-ji was a simple man. As long as he lived, he continued his business of changing money. He was fond of keeping cows and would himself travel to Gwalior to buy them. Cows from Gwalior were famous for the quantity of milk they produced and were also very gentle and good-mannered. They could be milked even without a calf, and one didn't need to tie a Gwalior cow's legs while milking it. As a young kid I would drink milk straight from a cow's udder and never come to any harm. These cows were most pleasant to look at too. Dada-ji would regularly bring me milk to drink. He loved to play the game of eighteen dices (*baghiya baghha*), and every evening he visited the Shiv temple and sat there for two hours singing bhajans. He passed away at about fifty-five years of age.

My father strictly supervised my education from the very beginning, and I was beaten by him at the slightest of mistakes. I vividly remember that when I was learning the Nagari alphabet, I could not write the letter 'उ' even after much practice. That day, Pita-ji left for the court and I too went off to play. When he returned, he asked me to write 'उ' and I couldn't. He found that I had sneaked out to play and as punishment he beat me with the iron butt of a gun. The beating was so ferocious that the metal twisted. I ran to Dada-ji to save myself. Nonetheless, I remained stubborn and defiant even from a very early age, in spite of my father's strictness. Once, I destroyed all the peaches from a tree in a nearby orchard belonging to someone else. The gardener chased me but couldn't lay hands on me. He complained to Pita-ji, presenting the wasted fruit before him. The beating that followed was so harsh that I couldn't rise from my bed for two days. This was a pattern—I was beaten black and blue but that did not deter me from mischief. Perhaps these blows received in childhood hardened and strengthened my body.

My Adolescence

I was fourteen years of age when I entered the fifth year of my Urdu class. I started reading novels with great interest and managed the money for them by stealing from Pita-ji's trunk. The bookseller knew my father and complained to him. The family started keeping an eye on me; I stopped buying books from that seller. Around the same time, I had picked up a couple of bad habits—smoking cigarettes and sometimes bhang. This, combined with the romantic ideas and temptations of Urdu novels and ghazal collections, changed me for the worse—a direct result of some money easily coming into my hands at an impressionable young age. The rot was just beginning to set in, but I was saved by God's grace. One night, high on bhang, I went to steal money from Pita-ji's trunk and, not being in control of my senses, closed the latch with a noise. Mata-ji got suspicious and caught me with the keys to the trunk. My personal trunk was searched and money found, along with the novels I had purchased with the money. All now knew of my secret and of the theft. The books were immediately torn into pieces.

I was caught, but this was a blessing in disguise, or else these bad habits would have ruined me. I again tried stealing, but Pita-ji changed the lock of the trunk. Then I started stealing from Mata-ji. I failed my Urdu middle-school examinations twice, and I then expressed my wish to learn English. Pita-ji was not keen on the idea and wanted me to join a business, but Mata-ji supported me. There was a temple which shared a wall with our house and had a resident priest (pujari). Around the time I failed the middle-school examination for the second time, I started frequenting the temple and interacting with the pujari. I was much influenced by him and even learnt some basic priestly rituals. The pujari impressed upon me the importance of *brahmacharya* (celibacy), and I saw him as my guide and mentor. And inspired by another person, I also started exercising regularly. The bad habits and the unhealthy mindset slowly melted away. But I couldn't give up smoking; in fact, I was still consuming fifty to sixty cigarettes in a single day. I was disappointed in my inability to give up this addiction. I joined the mission school in grade five for English classes, where I met my classmate Sri Sushil Chandra Sen. We became close, and his influence finally led me to give up smoking altogether.

With regular exercise, my body got stronger and my countenance improved. Observing my proclivity to pray and spend time in the temple, one Sri Munshi Indrajit, who too would visit the temple to meet someone, advised me to do *sandhya*. I was curious to know what sandhya meant. Munshi-ji explained the basic tenets of the Arya Samaj to me. I read *Satyarth Prakash*, which completely changed my life. I turned a new leaf by religiously following its teachings, and I especially followed the tough rules of celibacy. I would sleep on a blanket laid on a wooden cot and rise every morning at four. Then I would freshen up, perform sandhya, followed by exercise, but my mind was not at ease and remained unsettled. I further gave up eating at night and substituted dinner with a small glass of milk. Sometimes I would ejaculate while sleeping, possibly a reaction from the sudden giving up of bad habits. I was advised to give up salt, which I did, and my meals would consist of dal or saag without any salt, spices or chilli. For five years, I ate food devoid of any salt, which helped improve my health. Those around me were astonished at my transformation.

I soon became a staunch follower of the Arya Samaj, regularly attending their conventions and meetings, attentively listening to the sermons of the *sant*s and mahatmas. I would readily travel 3 or 4 miles to meet any sanyasi who happened to be visiting the town. I would serve them with the utmost humility for I was very keen to learn Pranayam; the sect or the denomination of the holy men did not matter. When I was in the seventh grade of my English school, a preacher from the Sanatan Dharma tradition, Pandit Jagat Prasad-ji, arrived in Shahjahanpur and began criticizing the Arya Samaj in his sermons. The Arya

Samajis protested and challenged him to a debate (*shastraartha*) with their representative, Pandit Akhilanandan-ji. The debate was in Sanskrit and left the audience much impressed.

The neighbours noticed my involvement in these activities and complained to my father. Pita-ji directed me to leave the Arya Samaj, for now they had been defeated in the debate. I answered, 'The teachings of the Arya Samaj are universal. Who can at all defeat them?' There were regular and heated arguments between Pita-ji and me on my participation in the Arya Samaj activities. He finally threatened to kill me in my sleep if I did not withdraw myself. I could either leave the Arya Samaj or leave home, I was told. I realized that our differences had come to such a point that Pita-ji might actually do something violent. I said it was better to leave home. I wore only a shirt and pyjamas. I was changing into a dhoti (wearing only a *langot* under it) when Pita-ji snatched the dhoti from me, ordering me to leave home immediately. I was furious. I touched his feet and walked out, not knowing where to go. I did not know many people in town who could have sheltered me, so I walked towards the jungle. I spent one night and one day sitting on a tree, eating green gram (chana) from the nearby fields and taking a bath in the river. The second evening I went to the Arya Samaj mandir to attend a lecture by Pandit Akhilanandan-ji. I was standing alone under a tree, quietly listening to the lecture, when Pita-ji turned up with two more men and took me away to the headmaster of my school. My headmaster was a Christian, and I explained everything to him. He advised my father to be more patient with me, for it was not appropriate to hit a grown and mature boy. He lectured me too. From that day, my father did not ever hit me. My leaving home had saddened every member of the family; they did not eat the whole day and were worried if their only son had met with an accident (drowned in the river or cut into pieces by a train). Now, Pita-ji became more tolerant of my views and did not offer any strong opposition to my actions. On my part, I paid attention to my studies and excelled in my classes. This was the situation till grade eight.

Once, Sri Somdev-ji Saraswati visited the Arya Samaj in Shahjahanpur. I was in grade eight then. His sermons were very influential among the citizens of the town, and they prevailed upon him to spend some time in Shahjahanpur. Swami-ji had been unwell for some time and the town's pleasant, healthy environment convinced him to extend his stay. A few medicines were prescribed to Swami-ji, and some other person expressed their sympathies, but that did not help Swami-ji very much. I would visit him regularly and spend a lot of time taking care of him, sometimes an entire day and night. This interaction was a life-changing experience for me. I was greatly impressed by his teachings and tried to implement them in my daily life. His teachings gave me inner strength, and I will write more about this a little later. He was my mentor and showed me the path of life.

Some young men organized the Arya Kumar Sabha in the Arya Samaj mandir, which met weekly on Fridays. They discussed religious books, debated and wrote essays on chosen themes. It was here that I learnt public speaking. Several members of the Kumar

Sabha would go to fairs in the city to promote the teachings of the Arya Samaj. In this process, there were arguments with the Muslims. The police, suspecting trouble brewing, stopped the preaching by the Kumar Sabha members. The Arya Samaj members tried to extend their control over the Kumar Sabha (to check their activities). But was it likely that these young men would follow anyone else's diktat? In response, the Arya Samaj was locked up to prevent the Kumar Sabha meetings from being organized. They were even threatened that if they tried to organize meetings there, the police would be called and the young men would be thrown out of the premises. For the next several months, we held the Kumar Sabha meetings in the maidan, but after a while it became difficult to sustain the *sabha*. It was eventually disbanded, much to the satisfaction of the Arya Samaj.

Our Kumar Sabha's work was known outside the town as well. The All Indian Youth Conference's annual meeting was held at the same time when the Congress session was scheduled in Lucknow. The members of Lahore and Shahjahanpur were the most awarded in this conference, and this found a mention in the local newspapers too. I became acquainted with a student of the mission school around this time; he would occasionally participate in the Kumar Sabha and was quite impressed by my speeches. Actually, he was my neighbour but there had been little interaction between us. Now, we spent some more time together and I came to know that he was originally from a village. And his village was known for the fact that nearly all its inhabitants kept rifles and pistols which were made locally in the village itself. These were capped rifles and pistols. Even this gentleman had a small single-barrelled pistol which he carried around with him in the town. When we became close, he offered the pistol to me to keep. I had really wanted to keep a weapon, because my father had several enemies who had once even attacked him with sticks. I imagined killing them once I laid hands on a pistol. While my friend carried the pistol around with him, it had never been used. It proved to be utterly useless when I tried it out. I threw it aside. Our friendship continued to grow, and I would walk to his house in the evening to share the last meal of the day with him. He would accompany me to see Sri Swami Somdev-ji too. When his father returned home from the city, he disapproved of this. He warned me not to spend time with his son, nor to take him to visit others, and threatened to send goons to beat me up if I did not pay heed to his warning. I stopped visiting his home, but my friend continued to visit me.

I hadn't actually travelled on a train till I was eighteen years of age. Once, I bought a third-class ticket with my friends but travelled in the superior category interclass—an act that made me disappointed with myself. I had become very committed to the idea of speaking the truth and of being honest. I tried to convince my friends that this was a type of theft, and that we should pool money together and pay the difference in fare to the station master. In yet another instance, Pita-ji filed a court case, telling his lawyer to summon me whenever needed. The lawyer once called me to sign my father's name where it was printed in the official documents. I refused, saying that it was a sin. The lawyer tried to persuade me that this was a high-value case (of 100 rupees), and if he did not submit the signature that day the plea would be rejected. I was not moved and ultimately did not sign the papers. I continued to believe and practise the path of truth, no matter what the circumstances were. I do not hesitate in speaking the truth.

My mother was a constant support in my life—whether it was my interest in religion or my studies. She would wake me up at four in the morning for my daily *havan*. Mata-ji and Pita-ji travelled to Gwalior for my younger sister's marriage. I remained back in Shahjahanpur with Dadi-ji for my annual exams. I joined the wedding party as soon as the examinations ended. The *baraat* had already arrived, and even before I reached the venue, I received information that the baraat had prostitutes as dancing girls. I did not join my family at the wedding and did not attend any of the ceremonies. I requested my mother for some money. She gave me 125 rupees, with which I travelled to Gwalior and tried to purchase a revolver. I had heard that it was easy to buy arms in the kingdom. I searched extensively but only found capped rifles and pistols, none of which used cartridges. Eventually I did find a man who, in fact, conned me—I bought a capped revolver with five shots for 75 rupees from him. I also got some locally made gunpowder and caps from him. I was very pleased with my new gun and headed straight to Shahjahanpur. There, I loaded the revolver but nothing much happened; the shot travelled only about 15–20 yards because of the poor quality of gunpowder. So my adventure turned out to be a disappointment. When Mata-ji returned home, she inquired about my purchases with the money she had given. I answered in a roundabout way, to change the subject, and said that all had been spent. Possibly, a *ginni* was left, which I returned to her.

If I ever needed money, I would ask my mother, and she would readily give it to me. My school was about a mile away from home. I requested her for a bicycle, and she gave me nearly 100 rupees. I bought a bicycle. I was now in the ninth grade. If I wanted to read a book, whether related to religion or the nation, I always approached my mother for the money to buy it. My travel to Lucknow was also sponsored by her.

My father and grandfather did not approve of my travelling to attend the meetings, but I was very keen on participating in the Lucknow Congress. About the same time, the Sewa Samiti in Shahjahanpur began its work. I was an enthusiastic volunteer in it. Again, while my father and grandmother did not like my involvement in such forums, my mother never discouraged me. They also wanted to marry me off, but my mother insisted that I should complete my education first and only then think about marriage. As a result, she would have to bear the brunt in the form of scolding and punishment meted out by Pita-ji. Indeed, it is Mata-ji and Gurudev Sri Somdev-ji who have shaped my life. The strength and fortitude of my character comes from Mata-ji, and it is her gift that I do not waver in my decisions in life.

Mata-ji

My mother arrived in Shahjahanpur as a married girl, merely eleven years of age. As a young girl she knew very little and was illiterate. My Dadi-ji invited her own younger sister to live with the family, and it was she who taught my mother how to run a household. My mother soon learnt how to cook and take care of the family. And she started to learn Hindi around five or seven years after I was born, out of her own interest and initiative. She learnt some basic reading and writing from her friends—the women in the neighbourhood who knew the alphabet, a little bit. Whatever little time she had left after her household duties, she would use it to practise her reading and writing, and in a while, with hard work and persistence, she began reading books in Hindi. It was my mother who taught my younger sisters in the initial years of their education, when they were still very young. With my involvement in the Arya Samaj, there was much that Mata-ji and I could talk about. Her views are now more liberal. If I didn't have a mother like her, I fear that I would have wasted my life, trapped in routines like most others. It was not only my education that she supported but also my revolutionary life, very much like Giuseppe Mazzini's mother did for him. I will write more about this subsequently. My mother's most important teaching for me was that I should not indulge in or cause loss of life, that I should never kill my enemies. And later in life, there were one or two instances where I had to break my pledge to honour her command.

My life-giver! I did not have an opportunity in this life to even attempt to show my gratitude to you. It will be impossible to repay my debts to you even if I have several lives. It is impossible and inadequate to describe in words the way your love and strength have shaped my life. I vividly remember each and every instance where your guidance redeemed me and showed me the path of serving the country. You were my guide in my religious interests, too. What little education I have, I owe to you. Even if you wished to scold me, it was done in a gentle manner; if I was arrogant and adamant, you still told me, with patience and love, to think about the adverse consequences of my actions. I think of you, your enlightened words, and I bow my head to you. You did not allow me to lose patience even in the most trying circumstances. Your sweet, gentle guidance was always a comfort to me. I did not encounter any hardship in life all because of your kindness. Guided by your life and teachings, I did not aspire to any material comforts or riches in this life.

Janani! You gave me this life and nurtured me, body and soul. I pray that I have you as my mother for all my lives to come. I do have one wish, that I have the opportunity to serve you, and then I would consider it a successful life. My wish will not come true, and you will receive the news of my death. Ma, I am confident that you will take pride and courage in knowing that your son gave up his life for the most supreme, the greatest of all mothers, Bharat Mata. My resolve to serve my country was unshakeable and I sacrificed my life for Bharat Mata—I did not sully your womb. When the history of independent India is written, your name will find pride of place on one of its pages. Guru Gobind Singh's wife received the story of her sons' sacrifice with joyous fortitude. *Janm Datri!* Bless me, so that I have the strength to face death, so that I embrace it with joy, thinking of you and of God.

My Gurudev

Besides Mata-ji, whatever I made of my life was due to the blessings of the most revered Sri Swami Somdev-ji. Your name was Sri Brajpal Chopra, and you were born in Lahore, Punjab. You came from an illustrious family; your grandfather was one of the ministers of Maharaja Ranjit Singh. Your mother died soon after you were born and it was your grandmother who raised you. You were the only child. As you grew slightly older, your aunts tried (twice or thrice) to poison you so that your share of the property would revert to their sons. But your uncle was especially fond of you and took particular care of your education. You studied in English schools just like your cousins. You appeared in the entrance examinations and were ranked first when the results were declared, while your cousins failed. Your family, when they received this news, was as if in mourning; no food was prepared that day. No one praised you; they did not even ask you if you were hungry, and they all looked at you with hatred and contempt. You were already sensitive to their mistreatment, but this episode especially hurt you.

You joined college after your uncle persuaded you, but you were not happy to remain detached. You were a kind-hearted person, and would give away your own books and clothes to your classmates. In fact, you gave away the new clothes you received and continued wearing the old, worn-out ones. Your uncle was chided by the neighbours a couple of times over why he didn't provide you with new clothes. He, in turn, was surprised because he had done just that. Your uncle then checked your belongings and, finding only worn-out clothes, asked you what you had done with the new ones. When you explained what had happened, he understood and said that you should simply ask for new clothes to be distributed among your needy classmates, and that there was no need to give away your own. You provided food at your home to some of the poorer classmates. But you continued to remain unhappy and disturbed by the unpleasant behaviour of your aunts and cousins. That was why you never married. You decided to give up home; one night, when all were asleep, you quietly walked away. You left home empty-handed. Several days were spent wandering, and you eventually found yourself in Haridwar in the company of a *siddha* yogi.

The seeker had found what he sought! You stayed there gaining initiation into Yoga Vidya. And under the guidance of your guru, you could now maintain a state of samadhi for eighteen to twenty hours. You lived here for many years, acquiring expertise in Yoga Vidya, to the extent that you could make your body very light and walk on water as if it were solid ground. You became interested in travelling and studying more. For this, you arranged for scholarly books on the *shastra*s and continued to study and travel simultaneously.

When Lala Lajpat Rai was punished with exile, you were in Lahore and submitted a declaration to a newspaper. Those days, the deputy commissioners would not accept any declarations for publication in newspapers, but this one was most impressed after meeting you. He approved its publication. This piece appeared as 'A Warning to the British' (*Angrezon Ko Chetawani*) on the front page of the newspaper. The declaration was so audacious and provocative that the newspaper was immediately sold out. They had to issue a second printing on popular demand. The deputy commissioner summoned you. He was seething with anger; in one instance he would look at the newspaper held in his hand shaking with fury, and in the second instance he would slam his hand on the desk in frustration. But he could not say anything. The text of the declaration was something to the effect that if even now the British failed to mend their ways, then those days would not be far when there would be a repeat of the scenes of 1857—when British children were killed and their women dishonoured. And the concluding line was: 'But this is all a dream, merely a dream.' It was because of these very lines that the deputy commissioner could not take action against you.

One of the places you travelled to was Bombay. The people here were mesmerized by your lectures, and one of the people who was greatly moved was the elder brother of Maulana Abul Kalam Azad. He invited you to his home. You were clad in a simple dhoti and kurta, with a *safa* tied on your head; you had not yet started wearing saffron robes. Maulana Azad's ancestors had come from Arabia, and his father was well settled in Bombay. He lectured on religious texts and had a large following in the city. This gentleman (the brother of Maulana Azad) was so influenced by you that he altogether stopped going to his father's gatherings (religious sermons). He would spend most of his time with you, and when you would gently ask him to leave he would get emotional and tear up. He would say that he did not wish for anything in this world except to learn from you. Once, you were a little cross with him and lightly tapped his head with your palm, in a mock gesture of hitting him. But he was so affected by it that he spent his entire day sobbing. His own family and followers tried to persuade him to rejoin the religious lectures. His stubborn refusal even angered them; they said that he had fallen under the spell of a kafir. One evening you went alone to the seashore for a stroll, and you were surrounded by armed men, who had come to kill you. Upon receiving this news, he realized that your life was in danger, and he urged you to leave Bombay. One early morning, you received a telegram at a railway station which bore the tragic news of the suicide of Maulana Azad's brother. You were deeply saddened by it. In later years, even the memories of this episode pained you. One evening, when I was sitting by your side, I heard you sigh deeply. It was rather dark, but I saw that you had tears running down your face. It was only after I pleaded with you for several hours that you shared this story of your association with him and his untimely demise.

You were fluent in English and had an excellent foundation of the shastras. You were also an outstanding and fearless orator. You represented the Madras Congress Committee at the All India Congress Conference. Raja Mahendra Pratap-ji was much impressed by your speech at the annual gathering of the Arya Mitra Sabha of Agra. Raja Sahib touched your feet and hosted you at his home. Since then, he has been your follower and listens to your lectures regularly. He would say: one seldom comes across such a daring speaker. I first heard you in 1913, when you visited Shahjahanpur for the annual gathering of the Arya Samaj. You used to stay in Bareilly then. And you had become very weak because of an unidentified illness.

You would lose blood during bowel movements—sometimes a few drops, sometimes more. You did not suffer from haemorrhoids. Some speculated that there had been a serious infection in the intestine caused by a faulty yoga asana. You had surgery, but it got worse, and you have been losing blood ever since. None of the medicines seemed to work. Despite being so frail, your voice was so powerful that when you lectured, it easily carried to people 3–4 furlongs away. You were regularly invited to Arya Samaj events, and I had the good fortune of meeting and associating with you in 1915, when you had stayed back in Shahjahanpur.

Swami-ji, you guided me on religious and political matters and encouraged me to read books on these topics. You were well informed on political issues and would regularly consult Lala Hardayal. You once rescued Mahatma Munshiram-ji (late Swami Shraddhanand) from the police, and you were close to Acharya Ramdev-ji and Sri Krishna-ji. While you discussed politics, you did not share everything with me. You would often encourage me to visit Europe after my studies—to see the motherland of Giuseppe Mazzini. The Lahore conspiracy case began in 1916, and I would closely follow its details in the newspapers. When the verdict was announced Bhai Parmanand was given the punishment of death by hanging. Bhai Parmanand's *Tawarikh-i-Hind* was a great influence on me, and this news greatly angered me. I realized that there is no justice in the British Raj—it was, in fact, most oppressive. I vowed to avenge Bhai Parmanand's death and to dedicate my life to the destruction of British rule in India. I shared the news of the verdict of the Lahore conspiracy case and my intent to do something about it with you. You, too, were angered and saddened by it. You cautioned me that while it was easy to make a pledge in an emotional state, it was far more difficult to remain committed to it. I folded my hands before you, humbly stating that if I continued to have your guidance and blessings, then I would not waver in my path. From that day on, you seemed to have more confidence in me and would discuss political issues more freely. And it was that day that sowed the seeds of my life as a revolutionary. You considered the principles of the Arya Samaj to be supreme yet did not hesitate to learn from and refer to the teachings of Ramakrishna Paramhansa, Swami Vivekananda, Swami Ramtirtha and Mahatma Kabir Das.

You are the source of strength in my spiritual and religious endeavours. All that you had predicted about my future years literally came true. You would say that this body is mortal, and you would not be around when I needed your help. If you had survived, you would have guided me towards living an ideal life. It was my misfortune that I could not improve my yoga under your guidance. In your last days you tried to teach me some techniques of yoga, but your body was so weakened that even the smallest of efforts led you to lose consciousness. You lamented that your yoga skills had been destroyed. And advised me to stay near you during your last breath, and said that, if possible, you would be able to tell me where your next birth would be. Despite such bodily weakness and losing blood on a daily basis, you were never sad for your own self. Neither did your voice lose any of its power. And your writings were as powerful as your speeches. One of your followers had collected some of your essays and books, but these were destroyed. Some were with Sri Swami Anubhanandan. Some essays have been published.

You left this world at the age of about forty-eight. I would like to recall some words of Mahatma Kabir Das, the ones which most moved me and seem poignant at this juncture:

> *Kabira shareer sarai hai bhada deke bas*
> *Jab bhathiyari khush rahae tab jeevan ka ras.*

(Kabir says, this body is an inn, which you
inhabit by paying rent.
You experience the essence of life when the
innkeeper [the soul] is happy.)

> *Kabira kshudha hai kukari karat bhajan mein bhang*
> *Yako tukra dari ke sumiran karo nisank.*

(Says Kabir, hunger is like a bitch which
disrupts devotion.

Throw a piece of food to satiate it and continue
your prayer uninterrupted.)

Neend nisani meech ki utha Kabira jaag
Aur rasayan tyag ke naam rasayan chaakh.

(Sleep is a sign of ignorance, arise and awaken, O Kabir,
Give up all other delicacies, savour the name of God.)

Chalna hai rehna nahi chalna biswe bees
Kabira aise suhaag par kaun bandhawe sees.

(Twenty out of twenty [all without exception] are
transients in this world.
Why attach yourself to its attractions, O Kabira?)

Apne apne chor ko sab koi daare maari
Mera chor jo muhe mile sarbas daaru vaari.

(All tend to annihilate their own thief [corruptions]
I shall give up everything for the one who stole me.)

Kahe sune ki hai nahi dekha dekhi baat
Dulha dulhin mil gaye suni pari baraat.

(This happened before my eyes, it is not hearsay,
The bride and bridegroom have become one, their
wedding procession is irrelevant.)

Nainan ki kari kothari putari palang bichhaye
Palkan ki chikk daari ke pritam ley rijhae.

(Dark eyes are the lovers' chamber, pupils form the bed,
Eyelids are the curtains, all enticing the beloved.)

Prem piyala jo piye sees dakshina dey
Lobhi sees na dae sake naam prem ka ley.

(Those who drink the cup of love, must sacrifice
their head [ego]
The greedy cannot offer their head, only pay empty
service to love.)

Sees utare bhoi dhare taape rakhey paon
Das Kabira yun kahe aisa hoe to aav.

(Place your head on the ground and then your foot on it.
Says Kabir Das, if you are capable of this, only then are
you welcome.)

Nindak niyare raakhiye aangan kuti chhawaye
Bin paani saabun bina ujjwal kare subhae.

(Keep your critics close, give them space in your house,
They cleanse your character, without water and soap.)

The Vow of Brahmacharya

The current situation is such that the children and
the youth—a priceless treasure for the country—have
poor guidance in their life. The children of the rich are
nearly entirely brought up by servants hired by their
families. Even middle-class families, which are caught
up in the businesses and routines of their jobs, do not
have time to guide their children. As a result, servants
hired at very cheap rates are responsible for bringing
up kids, and they invariably corrupt them. If one or
two children are lucky and get better-quality servants,
then it is the neighbourhood which destroys them.

Whatever little remains is left to the mercy of all that happens in school and college. The youth in college waste money by buying medicines advertised in the newspapers. Ninety-five per cent of them end up with poor eyesight. Some wear spectacles because of weak eyes, others wear them as a fashion statement. Lusting after beautiful women becomes important for them; there is hardly anyone who doesn't boast of multiple lovers. I have heard such strange accounts that it is embarrassing to narrate them here.

It is so difficult to stay away from these corrupting influences that even those few students who consciously try to resist them remain distracted. They then think that perhaps it is all right to have a little fun, and if something goes wrong there will be medicines to help recover, or eating healthy food later will help. They are gravely mistaken. There is an English saying: Only for once forever!

This is to say that once we allow something, especially a negative trait, to be a part of our lives, then no amount of medicines can help us. Eggs, fish oil, meat, etc., are all quite useless. The most important aspect is to develop character. It is only right that the teachers and students realize the state of this country and, for its sake, improve themselves. It is the path of Brahmacharya which alone has the essence of all the energy of this world. If one does not follow Brahmacharya, then one's life is dull and without vigour. Knowledge, strength and intelligence are all gifts of Brahmacharya. Among the greatest men in the world most are those who have pursued the path of Brahmacharya. Just study the lives of Parshuram, Ram, Lakshman, Krishna, Bhishma, Jesus, Mazzini, Banda, Ramakrishna, Dayanand and Ramamurti to know of the magnificent tradition and strength of Brahmacharya.

Still, the youths who have picked up bad habits and have ruined themselves in the wrong company, and who may now be trying to improve themselves through good education, should not lose hope. Human life is the sum total of our continuous efforts. Our mind will have a variety of thoughts, and those which interest us the most will be the most dominant in our personality, our behaviour. And actions, when practised again and again, transform into spontaneous or natural elements of our personality. This training or effort is what constitutes our life and is visible as our habits, our nature. This effort may be of a positive or a negative kind. If we generate positive thoughts, our efforts will be positive, and if we have negative thoughts then our actions will certainly be negative. Our heart is full of desires, of many kinds, and humans live and put in efforts to fulfil those desires. Children are trained in the atmosphere of their home, under the influence of their parents. Secondly, the circumstances we live in, influence our actions. And thirdly, conscious training manifests as actions. The third is so powerful that it can dominate and overcome any other traits acquired through parental influence and circumstances. Each decision of our life is shaped by training or effort. This continuous effort makes our life easy to manoeuvre, making some acts effortless. Otherwise, we would find it very hard to navigate even daily life—for instance, writing, wearing clothes and reading. We have acquired these skills through practice, and life would be impossible if each time we did these activities we had to learn them afresh. A child learns to stand and walk through practice, after falling multiple times, but once one learns to walk, one may walk for miles. Some are even able to sleep while walking—like the men who have to wind the clock outside the boundary wall of the jail; they have to walk continuously for six hours and often take a nap while walking.

One is sure to succeed if one keeps one's inner thoughts pure, and strongly commits oneself to greater or higher thoughts. It is appropriate for a student or a young man who wishes to walk on the path of Brahmacharya to follow a daily schedule and pay particular attention to what he consumes. Read about great men and works which influenced them. Do not waste time with romances and novels. Do not idle away time. If a negative thought ever crosses his mind, he should immediately drink cool water and start walking, or go and have a conversation with an elder. Vulgar ghazals, couplets and songs (on love and desire) should not be listened to or read. Avoid the sight of women, and do not meet even your mother and sisters alone. Avoid touching or hugging beautiful classmates.

The student should leave bed an hour before the sun rises, undertake his daily toilet and then exercise or take a walk in an open ground for fresh air. He should take a bath about five to ten minutes before the sun rises and then meditate on God's name with complete concentration. Always use fresh water from the well for bathing. If a well is not available, then use warm water to bathe in winter and cool water in summer. Rub your body well with a rough towel after bath. Take a small quantity of food after puja. The best would be a porridge made of wheat with sugar or salt to taste, or even fruits, dry fruits and milk. Then spend some time studying, and eat food between ten and eleven in the morning. Give up eating meat and fish, spicy, sharp and sour items, or those with ghee and oil, and even stale food. Do not eat onion, garlic, red chillies, khatai made of raw mango, and spicy food. Your food should be *satvik*. Dry foods should not be eaten. As far as possible, vegetables and leafy green saag must always be a part of the meal. Chew your food well. Food that is too hot or too cold is prohibited. Rest briefly after returning from school or college, and then proceed to write for an hour. After this, go to play and also spend some time walking around the field. It is not desirable to walk around the chowk or the bazaar where the air is polluted. Inhale fresh, clean air. Go to the toilet in the evenings too. Spend a few minutes in meditation and then eat fruit. If possible, try to restrict the evening meal to only milk and some fruit. A heavy stomach causes ejaculation while sleeping. If the food is not digested properly or if the mind is full of impure thoughts and therefore unable to rest, semen is ejaculated while one is asleep. Sleep by half past ten at night, after praying. One must always sleep under an open sky. Do not sleep on soft, silky beds. As far as possible, use a wooden cot and cover it with only a blanket or a thick sheet. You can also sleep by nine or ten at night if you do not wish to pray in the evening. And then again arise early morning at half past three or at four; rinse your mouth, drink cool water, go to the toilet and then start the daily recitation. Exercise or walk briskly around the time of sunrise. *Dand baithak* (sit-up) is the most superior of all exercises. It can be done anywhere. Try the version taught by Professor Ramamurti, which is beneficial for students. It exercises the whole body in just a few minutes. Additionally, one may also practise *shirshasana* and *padmasana*, and keep pictures of great men and warriors.

2

Love for the Country

After the passing of Sri Swami Somdev (whose feet are worthy of worship), I entered grade nine at my school and started reading books on my country. I participated in the Sewa Samiti of Shahjahanpur with great enthusiasm. It was established by Pandit Sriram Vajpayee. I began to feel that I must commit myself to the service of others, and it also gradually dawned upon me that my countrymen were facing grave difficulties. The same year, my close friend and neighbour cleared his entrance exams and went on to study in college. The exposure and independence that college gave also stirred love for the country in him. That year, the annual session of the All India Congress Committee was organized in Lucknow. I, too, participated in it, met several people and got a better idea of all that was happening in the country. The general consensus was that we should do something noteworthy for the country to change the situation. That British rule is responsible for the state of the country and the distressing situation of the people, causing them misery. That is why this government must be overthrown. I contributed wholeheartedly to these discussions.

The news of the arrival of Mahatma Tilak for the session was doing the rounds, and this was why the extremists had turned up in large numbers. The president of the Congress had earlier been welcomed with great fanfare. And Lokmanya Bal Gangadhar Tilak's special train arrived the next day. There was a massive crowd at Lucknow railway station. Pandit Jagat Narayan-ji was the head of the reception committee. Other important members included Pandit Gokarnanath-ji and many from the moderate group. The moderates feared that if Lokmanya's entry and his procession went through the city, then he might be welcomed with greater fervour than even the Congress president. So they decided that as soon as he arrived, he would be put in a motor car and then taken to the venue from the outskirts of the city. This was terribly disappointing news for the youths who were eager to see him. One of the college students, who belonged to the MA class, spoke against the arrangement and insisted that Lokmanya must be welcomed into the city. I, too, spoke in his support. Many other young persons present there decided that as soon as Lokmanya Tilak arrived, he should be immediately taken to his vehicle and then in a procession through the city. When the train arrived, Lokmanya was the first to alight. He was quickly surrounded by members of the official welcome committee and swiftly taken to his car. Me and another student lay down on the road before the vehicle. People tried to talk us out of it, but we didn't pay any attention to anyone. And, inspired by our act, many other young students did the same. All of us were lying or sitting on the road before the vehicle. I was so passionate in my behaviour that I was barely able to speak coherently. I was simply crying and demanding that they 'drive the car over my body, if you must'. The welcome committee requested for the car which had been used for the Congress president, but it was not given to them. A young man slashed the car's tyres. Lokmanya-ji tried his best to persuade us that we should let go of this stubborn demand, but no one listened to him. Somehow, a horse-driven cart was arranged and the horses were let loose. We bowed our heads at Tilak-ji's feet, asking him to board the vehicle. The cart was pulled by the young men through the streets of Lucknow. This was how Lokmanya was welcomed in the city. And one can hardly describe the response of the people. They were so excited that there was a clamour just to touch the vehicle in which Tilak-ji was travelling—this alone would make their lives blessed. The flowers which were showered on him and fell on the way were picked up by women and tied into their *pallu*s. People picked the dust off the ground where his feet had made contact and smeared it on their foreheads. Some tied the dust in their handkerchiefs. There was hardly any other leader who may have received a comparable welcome. The moderates were publicly embarrassed.

Revolutionary Movement

While in Lucknow, I came to know of a secret society which operated with the sole purpose of revolutionary activity against the British. I was drawn to their work and began participating in their activities. I became a member through a friend's reference and was soon part of their working committee. The society had little money but also needed weapons. As I returned home, I thought that perhaps some funds could be generated by publishing and selling a book. But where would I get the money for publishing the book? I thought of a scheme. I asked my Mata-ji for some seed money to start a business. She gave me 200 rupees. The manuscript titled *How Did America Win Its Independence?* was ready. We needed some more money to publish it, and I again asked my mother for help. She gave an additional 200 rupees. Out of the total money I borrowed from her, I returned half, after some copies of the book were sold. I still owed her half the amount and there were still many unsold copies left. At the same time, a pamphlet titled 'A Message for Countrymen' was released as a response to the arrest of Pandit Gendalal-ji along with members of the Brahmachari group in Gwalior. All the youths pledged to work tirelessly to spread their message. The pamphlets were distributed and pasted on walls in many districts. The United Provinces government seized both the book and the pamphlet.

Purchasing Weapons

Most people assume that everyone keeps weapons like revolvers, pistols and rifles in the princely states and there is no licence required for guns, etc. And that it is very easy to obtain these weapons. It is true enough that one doesn't need a licence on weapons in these regions and anyone can own a weapon, but guns with cartridges are owned by few because one needs permission from the police to buy cartridges or foreign gunpowder. There are no shops in the region where one can walk in and buy cartridges or weapons which use cartridges. Not even gunpowder or caps for capped guns are available, and all these need to be ordered from outside. These also need a permit from the Resident (who is the representative of the British government in the princely states). One cannot buy weapons or anything related to weapons without his permission. To avoid this surveillance and bureaucracy, capped guns are made locally. So is desi gunpowder, which is made out of saltpetre, sulphur and coal. The caps are smuggled in, and when that is not possible, a substitute of potassium sulphate (*mansal*) and potassium chloride (potash) is used. These are powdered separately and then mixed. Despite there being no prohibition on keeping arms, it is usually only the very rich or the zamindars who own capped guns or small revolvers. And they use local gunpowder, which absorbs moisture easily and becomes damp and therefore useless. Once, I tried to purchase a revolver, naively believing that there must be a shop where I could simply walk in and buy what I needed. I searched high and low but couldn't find anyone advertising the sale of weapons.

Then, I hired a tanga to take me around the city. The driver asked, 'What are you looking for?' I told him, albeit quite apprehensively, of my intent to buy weapons. After two or three days of searching the city, he managed to get me a capped revolver and some locally made gunpowder. I knew almost nothing about these things—I had purchased only 2 sers of gunpowder, kept in a trunk at home, and during the rains it became damp. I was very disappointed. The next time I set out to buy weapons it was after I had become a member of the revolutionary society. With the consent of other comrades, I took 200 rupees and began looking. After much effort I found a *kabaadi* shop which had a few swords, daggers (*khanjar* and *katar*) and capped guns. I gathered my courage and asked him if he sold those, and when he replied yes, I started examining them more closely and asked him for the price. I further asked if he or anyone else sold weapons with cartridges, and then he told me the whole story which I have shared with you. I bought two single-barrelled capped pistols and a katar from him. He offered that if I intended to visit again, he would try to procure weapons with a cartridge. I did visit again, partly because of my desire or greed to procure more weapons but also because we don't have any other avenue for buying those. He presented a beautifully made cartridge revolver. He also had a few old cartridges. It was an old revolver but of a very high quality. For this piece, I paid nearly the price of a brand-new one. The *kabaadiwala* was now convinced that I bought weapons on a regular basis. He made special efforts to procure weapons and managed to get some revolvers and a few rifles. He also made a neat profit off them, around 20–30 rupees on each item.

After some time, about two or three members of our organization together went to his shop. The kabaadiwala was prepared—he had repaired and improved some used weapons to sell to us. And he completely fooled us. We knew very little about these things. It was only after handling them several times did we learn a little bit. We also met another *sikligar*. He himself did not know much but promised to put us in touch with some rich people who owned weapons. Once, he connected us to a rich man who had a revolver, and we expressed interest in buying it. It was a new piece, and he asked 150 rupees for it. After much negotiation, he agreed to give the revolver and 100 cartridges for a sum of 155 rupees. One hundred went into his own pocket and 55 rupees was the commission of the sikligar. The revolver looked new and valuable, and we bought it. But we also thought it was impossible to keep buying things at these rates.

When we somehow managed to get a rate list for arms from dealers in Calcutta and Mumbai, we were taken aback. Except for one, all the guns and revolvers we had purchased until then had been at twice the official rate. The one we gave 155 rupees for was actually only worth 30 rupees, and 100 cartridges cost only 10 rupees. So we had actually bought items worth only 40 rupees and paid 155 rupees for them! We were rather deflated with this discovery. But what could be done then? We did not have any other way to get these weapons.

For the next round of weapon-buying, a group of three–four members went together, prepared with the rate list. Somehow, the police came to know of our plans. A police officer in disguise met me, promised to facilitate the purchase of many weapons and took me to a house. It was the house of the police commissioner, who, luckily for me, was not at home at that moment. I spotted an armed constable sitting at the entrance of that house, and he was known to me. Out of earshot of my companion, I asked him, 'Whose house is this?' When he answered, I quickly made a retreat. I returned and changed my residence to avoid being tracked. At that point of time, we had two rifles, four revolvers and two pistols. The secret police got a tip-off from the workshop where we got our weapons repaired that one of us would be visiting the shop today. All stations were informed and the trains searched. But the police were a little careless, and we made a narrow escape.

Losing money hurts. We got to know that a police superintendent had a rifle and that he was willing to sell. He was a pension-receiving Muslim. We met him and introduced ourselves as belonging to the *riyasat*. He asked us several questions to verify our credentials; after all, we were just young lads. He did not trust us and asked us to get an introduction letter from our area *thanadar*. I set out to get the details of the thanadar of the area where we claimed to be from. I also found out the names of a couple of local zamindars. Then I wrote a letter in their name, stating that I was the son of a zamindar of that area and that they knew me well. I signed the thanadar's name in English and the zamindars' names in Hindi. I gave the letter to the police officer who was selling the rifle. He carefully examined it and finally said that he would have to get this verified at the thana and that we would have to accompany him to the station to make a declaration that we were buying the rifle. We expressed our disappointment and said that we had already spent several rupees and put much effort into getting this letter—if this did not suffice then it couldn't be helped. But we would not go to the police. He was asking for 250 rupees for a rifle that actually cost 180 rupees. He was additionally giving 200 cartridges and the tools to fill it, which must be approximately worth 50 rupees. He was pretty much asking the price of a new item while selling an old one. We were willing to buy. He gave it a second thought—after all, he was getting the full value of the rifle. He was also old now and did not have any heirs. So, he took 250 rupees and gave us the rifle. No one went to the police. Around the same time, we got a revolver stolen from the house of a high official through one of his servants. We paid 100 rupees for it, though it actually cost 75 rupees, according to the list. We also arranged the theft of a Mauser pistol. It was a weapon we had always desired. It took us much effort to locate and obtain the Mauser. It officially cost 200 rupees at that time, and we purchased the stolen item for 300 rupees. And without a cartridge. Our old friend, the kabaadiwala, had five Mauser cartridges. These proved very useful. None of us had ever seen a Mauser and, of course, had no idea how to use it. It was with some difficulty that we understood its use.

We bought a total of three rifles, one twelve-bore, double-barrelled cartridge gun, two capped guns, three capped revolvers and five cartridge revolvers. We also bought ammunition (50–100 cartridges) for each weapon. All of this cost us about 4000 rupees. Additionally, we had a small number of swords and daggers.

Mainpuri Conspiracy Case

While we were busy organizing and planning our revolutionary activities, one of the members based in Mainpuri began fancying himself as a leader. He formed a separate organization and even collected some arms and ammunition. He ordered a comrade to arrange a robbery at a relative's houses to arrange for some quick funds. The latter did not respond or comply. He was then given a notice and a death threat. He promptly went to the police and the whole plan was exposed. The police nabbed the members of this unit. The news also reached us.

A Congress session was about to be held in Delhi. We planned to sell our book *How Did America Win Its Independence?*, the one which had been seized by the UP government, at the venue. On the occasion of the Congress session, I took the members of the Sewa Samiti of Shahjahanpur along with my ambulance unit and staff. The ambulance staff had permission to enter everywhere without being stopped. Young men stood outside the pandal, holding copies for sale and announcing, 'The book seized in UP: *How Did America Win Its Independence?*' The secret police surrounded the Congress camp. Right across was the Arya Samaj camp, where the police began searching the stalls selling books. I instructed my volunteers to stay put at the Congress campus entrance and not to allow any policeman to enter without permission from a minister of the welcome committee or the president of the session. I entered the Arya Samaj camp. All our books, about 200 in number, were in a single tent. I collected them in my overcoat, slung it over my shoulders and walked past the policemen out of the camp. I was in uniform, wearing a cap, and a large badge (of ambulance staff) was visible on my arm. No one was suspicious, and the books were saved.

We returned to Shahjahanpur from Delhi. There, too, police raids occurred. We moved places to a different house in another town. At around eleven in the night, the landlord closed the main door, locking us in. One of our comrades arrived and found the gate locked, and he called for us. We, too, became suspicious. We all climbed the wall and escaped. It was a dark night. We had only walked a few steps when we suddenly heard a command, 'Who goes there? Stand still!' We were a group of seven or eight people and understood that we were surrounded. We tried to take another step but again the voice rang out, 'Keep standing, or we will shoot!' We all stood. A police *daroga* appeared, with a pistol on his shoulder and a gun pointed at us. He had several constables with him. He asked, 'Who are you? Where are you off to?' We answered that we were students, on our way to the railway station. 'Where will you go?' 'Lucknow.' It was two in the night, and the train to Lucknow was due at five in the morning. The daroga was not convinced. A lantern was brought. He shone it on our faces and became less suspicious. He said, 'You must carry a lantern when walking about at night.' 'Yes, we are sorry, please excuse us.' We went on our way, saluting him respectfully. We came across a shack in an orchard and decided to wait there. It started to rain heavily. It was the month of January and bitterly cold. We were drenched and even the ground was filled with water. We spent the night soaked and freezing in the rain and cold. It was most painful and uncomfortable. We managed to dry our clothes next morning at a dharamshala. The following day, we came to Shahjahanpur, buried our guns in the ground to conceal them and then reached Prayag.

Treachery

We stayed at a dharamshala in Prayag for two or three days. It was decided that one of our members was a person of weak character and he should be killed. If he were caught, then everyone else would be in trouble.

I protested, 'It is not right to kill another human being.' But the majority opinion was that he should be done away with the next day. I remained silent. There were four of us together, and a little later in the afternoon we decided to visit the fort at Jhansi. We returned in the evening, crossed the Ganga and arrived on the banks of the Yamuna. After completing my toilet, I sat on the sand to pray and meditate. I was a little away from the edge of the water, on a higher ground. One of my companions remarked, 'Why don't you sit closer to the river?' I did not respond or move and kept sitting where I was. The three of them also came and sat near me. I closed my eyes and concentrated. A few minutes later, I heard a clapping sound and thought it must be one of us saying something. And suddenly a gunshot rang out. The bullet whizzed past my ear. I immediately realized that I was the target of the bullet. I pulled out my revolver and moved forward. I turned to see one of them aiming the Mauser at me. He was the same person I had argued with a few days back, but I was under the impression that we had resolved the issue. Still, he was there trying to kill me. I faced him. He ran away after firing the third shot.

The other two who were staying with us in Prayag also ran away with him. There was a moment's delay in me pulling out my revolver because it was kept in its leather cover. If any of them had remained for another thirty seconds or so, they would have been shot by me. I did not wish to waste my bullets by firing after all three ran away. I left. I had narrowly escaped and was lucky to have survived after being shot at from 2 yards away by a Mauser. And that too when I was sitting. I could barely comprehend how I had managed to come out of this episode alive. I was overcome with emotion and gratitude and started chanting God's name. I lost consciousness for a minute. The revolver and its cover both fell from my hands, and if at that point anyone wanted to kill me, they could easily have. I was still upon the ground when I heard a voice calling me, 'Arise!' I got up, picked up the revolver (and forgot the cover). I was wearing only a coat and a *tehmad* and did not have any shoes on. My hair had grown. Where could I go in such a state? Many thoughts raced through my mind.

I walked along the bank of the river, with my mind full of these thoughts. One of the things I considered was returning to the dharamshala, breaking open the lock and reclaiming my belongings. On second thought, it seemed an unwise thing to do—there may be a gunfight and a waste of life. Not an appropriate time for that. It was also not a good idea to seek revenge all alone—much better to get a few comrades along. I had an ordinary friend who lived in Prayag. I borrowed a cloth sheet from him with some difficulty and then took the train to Lucknow. I had money, so I got a haircut in Lucknow and bought a set of dhoti-kurta. Even if I did not carry cash, I would have managed because I always wore a gold ring, worth at least 40–50 rupees. I met the other comrades in Lucknow and narrated the whole episode to them. Then I went off into the forest to spend some days there, even wishing to turn to *sanyas*. The world meant nothing to me. Subsequently, I paid a visit to my Mata-ji and shared my experiences. She instructed me to go to Gwalior. In a few days, Mata-ji and Pita-ji all arrived at Dadi-ji's brother's house in Gwalior. I too was there.

The desire for revenge was burning inside me—it was all that I could think of. I even stepped out with my revolver one day with the intent to kill the enemy, but was not successful. This intense feeling and constant anxiety caused fever. I was ill for several months. Mata-ji understood what was gnawing at me. She spoke to me kindly, persuading me to give up the idea of killing the man who had shot at me, 'Promise me that you will not kill the man who tried to murder you.' When I hesitated, she said, 'I want this promise against the debt a son owes his mother. What is your answer?' I said, 'I have already sworn revenge.' Mata-ji compelled me to break my vow for revenge. She stood her ground, and I had to bow my head in submission. From that day on, my fever abated and I was better again.

Life as a Fugitive

I starting wearing clothes like the villagers around me. I also began working in the fields and paid particular attention to this work. Any onlooker would have figured out that I had lived in the city, perhaps even received a little education. I was already well-built; in a few days I was transformed into a farmer. It is not an easy task to till the land here—it is an extremely hard surface and few trees grow here. There is babul, neem and maybe a mango tree or two, the rest is barren land. The ground is full of thorns (of the *jharberi* bush) and every time I walked to the fields, my feet would be badly injured. Initially, I found it unbearable but gradually got used to it. Soon, I was ploughing as much land as any able-bodied man in the region would do on average. Working in the fields darkened my complexion so much that when I visited Shahjahanpur, no one could recognize me. I missed the train and reached Shahjahanpur at night walking on foot. During the day, when I was walking across the city, a policeman recognized me. He immediately went off to call the other men on duty. I ran. I was already tired from the previous day's 20-mile trudge. That day, too, I covered 35 miles on foot.

My parents helped me in this situation. I had already used up Mata-ji's savings. Pita-ji received an order from the government that his absconding son's arrest warrant would be executed by selling off the property that I had inherited from my grandfather. My father was so scared that he sold off his house and belongings and left Shahjahanpur. The house which was worth 2000 rupees was given away in only 800 rupees, and everything else too was sold off in distress. Whatever remained was spent in marrying off my two sisters. My parents were once again living in near-penury. The other members of the society, who too were on the run, were faring badly. For months, they ate nothing but gram and survived on a few rupees given by friends. They didn't even have proper clothes to wear. In desperation, they had to sell off our guns and revolvers. They had little choice and couldn't really look for work or say anything to anyone for fear of being arrested.

During this time, I thought of starting a business. I had learnt Bangla in memory of my classmate and friend, the late Sri Sushil Chandra Sen. When my younger brother was born, I named him Sushil Chandra after my friend. I thought of publishing a book series—translations from Bangla to Hindi. I believed that it would bring in some money and it was also a worthwhile pursuit. But I had no experience. I started translating the Bangla book *Nihilist Rahasya*.

Now when I think of it, it is rather amusing. I would herd some cows, bulls and buffaloes towards the barren lands and had nothing else to do while they grazed. So, I carried a notebook and pencil with me and used this time to translate. If the animals strayed too far, I would drop my notebook and chase after them to bring them back. I even spent a few days in a sadhu's hut, where I had more time to translate. I would carry wheat flour for four–five days and prepare my food at his hut. When the Hindi text was ready, I published the book with the title *Bolshevikon Ki Kartoos* (The Bolsheviks' Bullets) under the series called Sushil Mala (Sushil Series). The next book was *Mann Ki Lehar* (The Heart's Wave). I lost about 500 rupees in this publishing business. When the government announced the pardon and release of political prisoners, I thought of returning to Shahjahanpur and doing some work to help out my parents. I had been convinced that I would not be able to roam freely in Shahjahanpur ever again in my life. But with God's blessings it did happen. I returned to Shahjahanpur.

Pandit Gendalal Dixit

You were born in village Mai, on the banks of the Yamuna, near Bateshwar. You had studied up to the tenth grade in English and you were a teacher at DAV School, Auraiyya, Zila Itawa. That was when you founded the Shivaji Samiti, which emulated Shivaji's actions, of organizing groups, collecting money, buying weapons and distributing them among the members. You were once working towards this objective and transporting weapons from the princely state, but because of carelessness shown by some young members of the group, you were arrested near Agra station. You were brave and full of zeal and enthusiasm, so much so that you could barely sit still. You kept up the spirits of the youth by regularly addressing them, conversing with them. And for days you would not take off your uniform and boots.

You had the misfortune of getting arrested when you visited Brahmachari-ji to ask for his help. Brahmachari's group had raided many locations in the British territory, and after each raid they would return to hide in the ravines of Chambal. The British got in touch with the maharaja of Gwalior to get his help in arresting this group. The government even sent the army, which remained stationed for a very long time at Agra Fort near Chambal River. The police had mounted forces patrolling the area, but the Brahmachari group was never afraid of them. They were caught due to treachery. One of the members of their group was bought over by the British. The group chose a site for raiding, and they had to make an overnight stop before their intended final stop. The group set up camp for the night; they were also tired from walking all day. The traitor in the group offered to get food for everyone, for one of his relatives lived nearby. He returned with pooris and everyone, even Brahmachari-ji, who always cooked his own food himself (sometimes relying only on roasted potatoes and taro), chose to eat pooris that one instance. He had consumed just one when his tongue started stiffening. Those who had eaten more rolled over and collapsed. The pooris were poisoned. The traitor started to walk away on the pretext of fetching water. Brahmachari-ji shot at him, and as soon as his gunshot rang, there was retaliatory fire from all directions. They had been surrounded by the police, who were hiding out of sight. Brahmachari-ji took many bullets and was severely wounded. A pellet hit Pangelal-ji's left eye, and he lost sight in it. Out of eighty men, about twenty-five to thirty died, some from poisoned food, others from bullets. Those who remained alive were captured and locked in Gwalior Fort. Pandit-ji wrote a letter narrating this episode to us when we visited him while he was captive in the fort. Once, the three of us also came under suspicion while visiting the fort, and we made a narrow escape with the help of an officer.

Pandit Gendalal-ji was summoned from Gwalior when the inquiry into the Mainpuri conspiracy began. His health had suffered while in captivity in Gwalior and he got tuberculosis. He had to stop eleven times while making the journey between Mainpuri station and the jail to catch his breath. When the police started questioning him, he retorted, 'Why have you arrested these young children? I will tell everything.' The police were convinced and removed you from the jail and placed you near other government informers or witnesses. After observing everything closely, Pandit-ji made an escape from there with one of the witnesses. They found a room in a village and took shelter there. His companion went out on the pretext of going to the bazaar but never returned. He also locked the door to the room from the outside. Pandit-ji remained locked in it for three days without food or water. He was convinced that his companion had met with an accident or must be in grave difficulty. He finally managed to get himself out of the room, but he had not a single paisa on him. All the money had been taken by the other person. Pandit-ji walked from Kota to Agra and somehow reached his home. He was very unwell. His father thought it better to inform the police so that the family would not face any harassment. Pandit-ji pleaded with his father to let him remain for a couple of days and then he left home. He desperately searched for the three of us but got no information. He then took up a job of distributing water at a *piau* (drinking water fountain/point). He was growing weaker by the day, and he called over his wife and younger brother. The brother was clueless as to how to handle the situation. He was unable to help in any way. He set off his sister-in-law to another place and tried to get Pandit-ji admitted to a government hospital. My hand shakes as I write about the following events. Pandit-ji had left his earthly body by the time he reached the hospital. His lifeless body lay there alone. It is difficult to think of the utterly helpless circumstances in which Pandit Gendalal-ji Dikshit died. A great man who had selflessly served had died, and no one even knew of it. He had always wanted to die by a bullet. Your biographical sketch has been published in the monthly magazine *Prabha*. You were declared the key accused in the Mainpuri conspiracy case. One of the noteworthy things about this case was that of all the accused leaders, the police managed to capture only two. Out of these two, Pandit Gendalal-ji escaped with a government witness, and the other, Sri Shivkrishna, too escaped from jail and was never caught again. Those who were convicted were released after an official declaration. The secret police were extremely frustrated at these meagre results and much embarrassed in this case.

3

On My Own

After the government pardon, I reached Shahjahanpur and was met with unexpected hostility. No one would dare to even stand near me. If I approached someone, they would hastily fold their hands (in a namaste) and move away, avoiding any sort of contact. Police presence was all-pervasive and intimidating. They were still shadowing me, keeping a close watch on my actions and whereabouts. How long could I go on living like this? I began to weave cloth, but it was not easy to learn this skill. There were few weavers willing to teach me. The factory had a vacancy for the position of a manager. I tried to apply but the management asked me to first submit a safety deposit of 500 rupees. My situation was most pitiable. I had sworn not to beg for help from anyone and was even making do without food, sometimes continuously for three days. I had not even informed Pita-ji about my presence in the town. Where could I arrange 500 rupees from? I requested a couple of friends to give

200 rupees each, but they refused outright. This was a shocking experience for me and my whole world seemed to be engulfed in darkness. I did find a job after some time with the help of a friend. This improved things, and I had some money to live decently. And now, the same friends who had refused 200 rupees when I desperately sought their help were now leaving their money with me for safekeeping: bags of money with 4000 rupees in each of them, guns, licences, etc. This change in their behaviour with the change in circumstances amused me.

Time passed, and subsequently I met a few men whom I had admired. They too had heard a little bit of my experiences in the past while I was away from home. They were familiar with my writings, and were quite pleased to meet me. By this time, I had finished the manuscript of my third book, *Catherine*. I had also incurred substantial losses in my publishing endeavours. I suspended the publication of the 'series'. I submitted *Catherine* to a publisher and he printed it with a few minor changes. My close friends were delighted to see this book and encouraged me to keep writing. I wrote another book titled *Swadeshi Rang* (The Hues of Freedom), which was soon published.

I spent much effort in penning *Krantikari Jeevan* (Revolutionary Days). I showed it to many publishers, including in Agra, Kanpur, Calcutta, but none dared to publish it. They all returned the manuscript. My articles were published in monthly magazines under the pseudonym Ram or Agyat (anonymous). And these were received well by readers. I would use my spare time to pen down my thoughts and would simply send these off to the publishers. I mostly planned to translate from Bangla and English into Hindi. I also translated Sri Aurobindo Ghosh's Bangla book *Yogic Sadhan*. I shared the manuscript with one or two publishers, but they wanted to buy it at a very low price. These days, publishers have become arrogant because there is a large pool of writers and translators in Hindi. After much negotiation, a Banaras-based publisher agreed to print *Yogic Sadhan*. But before something could be done about this book, he closed his business and disappeared. There was no trace of the book. It was a good-quality manuscript and readers would have benefited from it. I had several copies remaining of *Bolshevikon Ki Kartoos* and *Mann Ki Lehar* which I gave away at a much-reduced price to one Sri Dinanath Sagtiya of Calcutta. I had managed to sell very few copies. This gentleman, Sri Dinanath, claimed the books without any payment. I requested him, sent a legal notice, and the court even imposed a penalty of 400 rupees on him, but I was unable to trace the whereabouts of Sri Dinanath. He had apparently left Calcutta for Patna and there too, he fooled several poor people, took their money and was absconding. I lost much and faced many difficulties because of my inexperience and there was no one to turn to for advice either. So, I wasted energy in these fruitless experiments.

Reorganization

Some known people approached me with the suggestion of reorganizing the revolutionary group. These were people I held in high esteem, but I was also much saddened by my past experiences. Noting my reluctance, they encouraged me and assured me that I would only have to guide and direct the group, the actual work would be done by the other members. They also claimed to already have a few keen people ready to join and said that there would not be any dearth of funds. I gained some confidence from their words and agreed. I also gave them my own weapons. They arranged a meeting between me and the leader of the existing group and praised him and his bravery highly. He was an illiterate, a village dweller. I understood that this was a ragtag bunch of selfish rogues, inclined only to create trouble. The leader requested me to guide their group's activities. There were some in the group who had returned from the army; they had been sent back from the war. I had never dealt with such a group. In the company of a couple of people, I went off to see their work.

After a few days, the leader of the group brought along a prostitute. He threatened her with a revolver so that she shouldn't attempt to leave. This episode caused a lot of anger among some members of the group who tried to contact me. At the same time, another member of the group, who knew the leader, was caught. As a result, the leader too was arrested, with some gold ornaments and a revolver in his possession. His bravery, of which I had been told many stories, unravelled before the police when he disclosed the names of his comrades and surrendered. Some thirty to forty men were captured—so much for his bravery.

There was another person who was truly brave. The police had been searching for him for a long time. One night, the police captain, accompanied by a few men on horseback and about thirty to forty armed personnel, surrounded his home when he was present. He went to the terrace and fired nearly 300 rounds at a go. The gun melted from the heat. But he successfully gave the impression that there were several armed men at the house. The police then hid themselves to take cover and waited for the sun to rise. That was when he took the chance to escape. He climbed out of the rear of the house. He was spotted by a constable, and he attacked the constable with his rifle butt. The constable cried out in pain, and that very instant a gunshot was heard from the house. The police thought that the constable must be mistaken and the man they were after was still in the house. Actually, he had instructed his wife to fire a shot if she heard anyone cry out. He was able to fool the police and escape into the jungles. There he joined another secret group. It so happened that even in the jungle, he came face to face with the captain of the police. Shots rang out from both sides and his foot was badly injured by pellets. By now he was bolder and wiser to the tactics of the police. But their group members were scattered, and they tried to take shelter with me. I got rid of them with some difficulty. They went back into the jungle and merged with another group. Soon after, the leader of that group shot them for misbehaviour. He, in turn, was shot by another one of his companions. In this manner, there was little left of the group. Those who were caught had several cases slapped on them. Some were imprisoned for three years, others for five and yet others for twenty years. One innocent soul who was not involved in any of the raids was caught in this because of personal enmity. He was hanged. And another man who had actually been deeply involved in these activities and had been found in possession of weapons and stolen goods, and had even been fired upon, was first convicted and punished to be hanged till death. But his sentence was reduced to five years' imprisonment after a court case, as he had found a competent lawyer to defend him. In cahoots with the jail authorities, he prevented any proper investigation into the dacoities. In this way, the group ceased to exist. Thank God my weapons were saved. Only a revolver was discovered and seized.

Printing Currency Notes

One of my friends met someone who could print currency notes. He had many ideas on how we could build on this scheme. According to my friend, this currency-note printer was a very competent person. I was very curious to see this process and expressed a desire to meet him. When this person met me, he was full of enthusiastic and encouraging ideas. I declared that I would provide the money and the place, and he should print. But this was to be done in my presence. I told him that I wanted to see him print currency notes, but he need not reveal the process to me if he didn't wish to. He decided to print a 10-rupee note first.

He asked me for a clean 10-rupee currency note. Out of that he took 9 rupees in the name of buying medicines. That night, all the preparation was done for making the currency notes: two pieces of glass, some paper, chemicals in a couple of glass bottles. The chemicals were mixed with water and plain paper was immersed in it. The clean note which was given by me was placed along with a plain piece of paper and both were washed in another chemical mixture. Then the note was wrapped in two plain pieces of paper made into a tiny packet. He then gave it to his companion to warm on a flame. The fire was a little distance from where we sat. His companion spent some time warming the packet and then came back with it. The note-maker untied the packet, placed the notes in between two pieces of glass, washed them in a chemical and laid them aside after tying the glass pieces together with a string. He declared that we should let it settle and the notes would be ready in two hours. We started chatting, discussing how printing notes involved a lot of expenditure; he promised to teach me the secrets of the process. I had to step out for some errand.

Following me, he too stepped out and we decided to meet again after a couple of hours.

I was deep in thought. How was it possible that a plain sheet of paper could be transformed into a currency note just by being kept alongside a printed one? I had learnt printing work at a press. I knew a little bit of photography too. And I had studied sciences. Still, I did not get an answer to my question. More importantly, how would the currency note get its serial number. I became highly suspicious of this whole affair. When I returned, after two hours, I was carrying a loaded revolver with me. The currency-maker also arrived. He removed the pieces of paper from between the glass and again washed them in a chemical. He finally unfolded them. One of the notes I had given and the other was kept exactly on top of it. I removed it and exclaimed, 'What a beautiful clean piece!' I took both the notes in my hand and compared the serial numbers. They were different. I confronted him. I told him that it might be possible to fool innocent, uneducated villagers or even unsuspecting literate people, but you couldn't fool me. I took out a piece of paper, wrote a declaration on it saying that he would never do this work again, and got him to stamp his fingerprints—of all ten fingers—on it. He seemed very reluctant to give his fingerprints. I pointed the revolver at him saying, 'This one works,' and he immediately put all his fingerprints on the declaration. He was shaking with fear. I had already spent 19 rupees on this. I kept both the notes, and all the material which he had brought to play this game on me. I thought I would show them to my friends. He disclosed that he had exchanged the tiny packet with another one when he gave it to his companion to warm over the fire. That was how they 'made' currency notes.

There exists a large gang that operates across the country, fooling people and profiting off them. I know someone who has made more than 50,000 rupees through this fraud. This is how it operates: They deploy agents who lure people with stories of printing money. And who does not want more money? So, people would readily agree and get notes made from these agents. At first, it would be a 10-rupee note, then a 100-rupee note, given by the duped person and then duplicated by the agent. And these notes were then used in the market, and they worked. And why not? After all, these were actual currencies which had been put there to fool people. Then the agent would ask for a higher-denomination note, say 500 or 1000 rupees, so that there was a greater profit. When the person produced such a note (often obtained with much difficulty), then the agents would disappear with the money. The person would keep waiting for them to turn up, but of course there was no trace of them. And when the glasses were untied, they revealed nothing but black pieces of paper. It was also not possible to complain to the police or share these details with anyone. If one did so, it was likely that the complainant would be caught and punished for participating in and abetting illegal activities. One could only wring one's hands in frustration. Some members of the gang were arrested by the police, but they were soon let off because they gave a commission to the police.

Deceit

Some of the members of the secret society drew up a document of rules and regulations for the group and brought it to me for my approval. It included a provision that members of the society who worked for it should get a monthly salary. I strongly disagreed with this. I was willing to allow the living cost from society funds for those who worked full-time for the group. But the society should only bear the expenditure for living, and not pay a salary. Even these people should be encouraged to generate their own income through finding work so that they do not become dependent on the society for all their needs or get reduced to being hands on hire rather than doing the group's work out of their own commitment. Hired men will not be able to bear the responsibility of people's lives, of maintaining secrecy—which are essential to the society's work. After hearing my views, those who had drafted this offered an alternative suggestion, that we should establish a fund for the group. Half of all the money that would be obtained from dacoities would be put in the fund for the running of the society, and the remaining half would be distributed equally among the members of the group. I was not in agreement with this either. And I refused to participate in the secret society's activities, which seemed to be aligned towards individual profit rather than a greater goal. When they saw my staunch opposition to their ideas, they began to plot against me.

They all had fallen silent. I was unable to understand why and how a group of people who claimed to look up to me, had approached me and pleaded with me to guide them and reorganize the group, were now reluctant to take my advice. They expected me to agree to their rules and regulations. I was most surprised. When I was associated with the Mainpuri case, all our comrades considered it a sin to use the group's money for personal expenses. In fact, we would ask our families for money for our personal use and then whatever amount possible would be contributed to the group's common fund. That is why I was unable to accept the terms proposed by this group of men. I thought that it was entirely possible that the group might get a large sum of money, and then its members may try to keep the maximum amount for themselves—a tendency which would lead to enmity. It would have serious consequences for the society. So I did not think it right to continue my association with these people.

They perceived that I would not budge and pretended to agree with me. In reality, they were scheming to deceive me and, if required, to even kill me. Three of them plotted a scheme to get rid of me. One of them, perhaps a little kind-hearted, revealed their plans to me. I was deeply saddened to learn of their intentions. These were men whom I greatly respected, and they were the ones plotting my destruction; they were willing to fall so low as to want to kill me through deception. The one who revealed this plan to me had done so because he wanted to keep a revolver with him and believed that I would trust him enough to give him the weapon. He demanded a revolver. I was aware that if I gave one to him, I would never get it back. And those days it wasn't easy to arrange for a replacement. I extracted myself from the company of these people with much difficulty.

Now, having removed myself from all kinds of distractions, I single-mindedly pursued my job. The plan was to save some money, earn some through commissions, and lend a hand to Pita-ji's business. My youngest sister was not yet married. Pita-ji was unable to arrange the money to see her married into a decent household. I managed to save money and arranged my sister's marriage into a zamindar family. Pita-ji's burden was relieved. Now it was only Mata-ji, Pita-ji, Dadi-ji and a younger brother in the family, and it was not difficult to manage among us. Mata-ji expressed a strong desire to see me married. There were several good matches brought to us. But I was sure that I should not enter into a marriage until I had a sufficient income. I left my job and set up my own business—a workshop for weaving silk cloth. A friend helped out with the funds. I worked hard and with commitment and by God's grace the business did well. Within a year and a half, the workshop gave a profit. I had started the business with an initial amount of about 3000–4000 rupees, and after one year I made a profit of around 2000 rupees. This was very encouraging, and I initiated a couple of other ventures. Around the same time, I received news that the revolutionary group in the United Provinces was being reorganized. The work for it had begun. I promised to contribute, but at that time I was neck-deep in running my businesses.

I gave myself six months to hand over the reins of the business to my partner and to disassociate myself entirely from it. Then I would be free to participate in revolutionary activities. And I did exactly that.

4

An Expanded Organization

Although I had earlier decided not to take part in the revolutionary movement, when the opportunity presented itself again I couldn't hold back. My thirst for revolutionary work had not been satiated and my dreams had remained unfulfilled. The Non-Cooperation Movement had lost its steam. We were hopeful that the youth that had participated in the Non-Cooperation Movement would now commit itself to the revolutionary movement. We reorganized ourselves and tried to mobilize the youth, but they appeared even more feeble than the dying movement itself. They were a disillusioned bunch. Their savings were over and so were the food stocks. They had little to look forward to in the future. In the Congress, too, it was the Swaraj group which seemed to have the upper hand. Those who had some capital and support of influential friends got into the councils and assemblies (legislative bodies). In such a situation, if the revolutionary groups had any money, they would have mobilized and worked with those who participated in the Non-Cooperation Movement. But no matter how sincere the commitment, everyone still has to eat to live. They at least need some food on a daily basis and clothes to cover their bodies. So there has to be an arrangement where the daily needs are taken care of. Some moneyed nationalists had contributed generously to the Non-Cooperation Movement. There were some sympathizers who would contribute a little bit in times of need. But we planned to reorganize on the level of the entire state, covering each district. At the same time, we had to keep away from the sight of the police. In such extraordinary circumstances, it was impossible to work by ordinary rules. We tried different things, but with little success. We appointed a unit in-charge in two or four districts, and for a few months we even gave them a monthly wage to meet their expenses. But this arrangement did not last more than five to ten months. Those who helped us with money, even if intermittently, stopped altogether.

We were badly off, and no one was ready to help us. All the responsibility of the group had fallen upon me. Those in charge of running the units in different districts were demanding money for meeting expenses. Several met me with their requests. I somehow begged for a loan and gave just enough to meet a month's expenses. Some of them were under debt themselves. I was unable to pay off debts. One of the members left when he could not get enough funds. I had nothing to offer him to make him change his mind or fill his stomach. It was a terrible situation. I somehow convinced the others to carry on.

In some time, we printed pamphlets with revolutionary messages. They were distributed all over the country on a specific date: Rangoon, Bombay, Lahore, Amritsar, Calcutta and the major cities of Bengal and all the districts of the United Provinces. Our pamphlets were circulating in all these places and the government was on high alert, hunting for the organization which had the capacity to distribute material on such a large scale on a single day. It was after this that I convened a meeting of the group's Working Committee and appointed someone to take up the responsibility of the districts where we had lost organizing members. The central group in the organization was also changed; we had to be cautious because some information about our members and activities in the United Provinces was already reaching the government. We planned our future course of action.

Difficult Conditions of Our Activists

Things were terribly difficult for our comrades. Even gram was difficult to get. Everyone was under debt. None had a single untorn piece of clothing. Some would pretend to be students and eat at the community kitchens of religious shrines. About four or five discontinued their work as district in-charge and left. I owed more than 500 rupees, which I had borrowed as a loan and spent. I was most unhappy seeing the situation of our comrades. I, too, couldn't eat a full meal. I appealed to a few sympathizers for loans but did not get a positive answer. I was perplexed and frustrated. I could not find a way out of this distressing situation. These kind-hearted youths would come, sit near me and ask, 'Pandit-ji, what should we do? How should we go on?' Just a glance at their distressed faces would make me cry; they had chosen the path of serving the nation and now they were in worse conditions than fakirs. The clothes on their bodies were in tatters; there was hardly a dhoti or a kurta on them which had not been kept together by extensive repairs. They would wear a langot during the day and cover themselves with an *angochha* while bathing. One meal of the day would come from the people among whom they worked and the second meal would be ground roasted gram (sattu) worth 2 paise. Ever since I was fifteen, I have been in the habit of drinking milk every day. But given the conditions of my young comrades, I did not have the heart to do that. So, I would also sit with them and eat sattu. Now that I had convinced these young men to give up their regular lives for a cause, I did not know how to sustain them. Where could I send them? We had grand plans and great enthusiasm when they all were made part of the movement. Many gave up their studies and committed themselves fully to the work. If I had any inkling that our situation would deteriorate so much, then I would never have participated in the samiti's work. I was in a quandary and did not know how to extract myself and the others from it. What should I do? I was desperate for a way out but could not think of anything. The only thing I could do was be patient, courageous and keep at the ongoing work.

The Bengal Ordinance was declared about the same time and several were arrested. This severely affected the morale of our young activists. We were quite helpless, unable to decide how to move forward. I tried to arrange a sum of 100 rupees which could be disbursed as a monthly wage. I requested and urged the representatives of each unit to collect donations on a monthly basis from the members and supporters, but none came forward. I personally approached a few people to contribute a part of their wage to our work, but they refused. I had the young members standing at my doorstep every day, demanding some money for meeting their basic expenses, for they were starving.

And I would get letters daily, saying the same. I even tried to place a few of them in jobs and businesses. Eventually, I had to shut down our units in a couple of districts, clearly telling them that we could not provide a regular wage. 'If you are in a position to explore other options, then you must do so, while doing the samiti's work, if you can. We will provide funds when we can, but we cannot promise a monthly salary.' Some would ask for a loan of 20 rupees, others for 50 rupees. Many left the organization in frustration. I could only say, 'Okay, I have done my best, if this does not suffice for you then I understand.'

Immaturity of the Youth Brigade

Some among us have an inflated sense of self, which is most detrimental to the movement. They strut about boasting of their achievements. If by chance, through a stroke of good luck, they contribute to a successful event, then they project it as if their role was of the greatest significance. They are able to convince the simple-minded of their courage, ability and efficiency, and the latter blindly believe them. The common people, especially the youth, are taken in but when it is too late, they find out the real scenario and feel utter disappointment. As the saying goes, they cook their one and a half grain of rice separately, that is to say, they try to carve out their own separate fiefdoms rather than contribute meaningfully to the movement. This leads to factionalism and the movement gets split into several groups. Such individuals are found in all walks of life, including in revolutionary groups. The youth are especially susceptible as they are easily excitable, lack patience to build something carefully. They handle a few weapons and begin to believe that they have taught the government a lesson. Even for me, as a young man, the greatest desire was to get hold of a revolver and kill ten to twenty British people. I see similar follies among the youth today. They too have a strong desire to obtain a weapon—it makes them feel powerful. When I asked them a simple question— what would they gain out of keeping a revolver?—they had no answer for it. I have seen many of them waste hundreds of rupees to fulfil this obsession—they are not part of a revolutionary group, they are not clear how they want to use it, but they still want to keep a revolver. A few such young men formed a society. It was led by a man who was of good character, self-respecting and sincere. This group claimed to have found a novel and relatively easy source of obtaining weapons. From here they could get arms as and when they desired and at a not-too-expensive rate. The weapons were also new. It was even arranged that if there was a steady payment initially, they could get some weapons in advance as well, to be paid for at a later date. With this plan, they could then get as many and whatever type of weapons they wanted, including machine guns. But this was the time when there was a series of fund crunches in the samiti. We would have liked to take advantage of this source and the terms they offered but could not do so without some initial seed money. Money was essential. But how was I to arrange it? No one was willing to donate or give us a loan. With no options left before us, dacoity was the only possible way out. But we were not willing to rob someone's personal property; if we must, let us rob the government. My mind was full of these ideas as I was travelling on the train one day. I was sitting close to the guards' coach. I saw the station master carry a small bag and deposit it in the guards' coach. There was a slight noise of opening and shutting and I stepped off my own coach to observe what was happening. There was an iron trunk on the ground, and I figured that the bag must have been kept in this. The same happened at the next station, where another bag was deposited in the trunk. I assumed that the iron trunk must be locked, tied to the rail coach with metal chains and would be unlocked when needed. A few days later, I was at the Lucknow station, where I saw coolies unloading the trunks full of money. On closer observation I realized that they were neither locked nor chained, as I had wrongly assumed. They were simply kept in the coach without any additional security measures. And I decided that I would grab these.

Railway Dacoity (Kakori)

I became obsessed with the idea. I checked the train timetable and estimated that between Saharanpur and Lucknow there must be approximately 10,000 rupees collected on the train. After verifying all the possible details, I gathered the members of our society. Initially it was proposed that about ten people should board the train when it stopped at a minor station, capture the station's telegraph office and remove the trunks, smash them and take away whatever money they could lay their hands on. But this operation required a large number of people. The alternative plan that was accepted was that the train should be stopped by pulling the chain when it was running between two stations. It was also decided that the chain must be pulled in the second-class and not the third-class coaches, because the latter were more likely to malfunction and not work at all.

On the day, all of us were on the train and when it stopped as planned, we all disembarked and reached the guards' coach. The trunks were removed from the coach. We first tried to break them open with a chisel, but those did not work and we used an axe. We instructed all passengers to climb back on to the train. The guard tried to climb back but we pinned him to the ground, ensuring that the train would not leave (without him aboard). Two of our men were positioned a little away from the track on the grass with instructions to keep firing shots regularly. One of our men disembarked from the guards' coach, carrying a Mauser revolver. He was clearly excited by this opportunity to use a Mauser and started shooting. When I saw this I immediately scolded him and asked him to stop—it was not his responsibility to fire while the operation was on. It was irresponsible, for loose firing may hit a passenger sticking his head out of the train. And that was exactly what happened: A passenger stepped out of the coach and was walking towards his wife, and he got shot and killed. I think it was because of our member's experiments with the Mauser, because by the time he removed the trunks from the coach and then stepped down from the train, two or three shots had been fired. That must be when the woman started crying from nervousness, which compelled her husband to walk towards her. And that was when he was shot because of my companion's irresponsible actions. Before we embarked upon this mission, I had drilled this point among all, that unless you are confronted by an armed person or someone is aiming a gun at you or someone shoots at you, do not fire on anyone. I did not want to murder anyone and make this mission a horrific sin. Despite my warnings, he did not stick to his job and ended up killing a man. Those comrades who were given the responsibility of firing shots were very skilled and experienced persons; it is impossible that it was their mistake. I saw that they were at their given positions, firing only every five minutes, as had been instructed.

We broke open the trunks and put the bags of money into three large sacks. I instructed them to check and re-check if anything had been left behind. This, too, was ruined by a man from our group. After running away from the train, we took out the money, put it in another bag and reached Lucknow with it. No one asked us who we were and where we came from. And in this way, ten men looted a train. That train had fourteen personnel who carried guns and rifles, and two armed British soldiers as well. But they all kept quiet. Both the driver and the engineer were scared stiff. They were both British. The driver lay prone in the engine and the engineer hid in the toilet. We had declared on the train that we would not harass the passengers; we would only take away the government's money. For this reason, the passengers also sat quietly through all this. They all were under the impression that some thirty to forty men had surrounded the train. In fact, a group of merely ten had created such terror in their hearts. Actually, people may find it difficult to believe that ten young men stopped the train and looted it. But that remains a fact. And most men out of these ten were about twenty-two years of age or younger and none of them was strongly built either.

I felt very confident after the success of this mission. My ideas had literally come true. I also had some idea of the so-called bravery of the police forces. The success of the train robbery created hope for future plans as well. The youth, too, were buoyed by the results of the plan. We paid off all our debts. Approximately 1000 rupees was distributed for the purchase of arms. The cadres were sent off to their respective centres, and we consolidated plans to start new centres for work. A youth organization got in touch with me and sought my help for making a bomb. I gave them some money and promised to send one of our members to assist them. But we made a few mistakes, as a result of which the whole group was scattered.

In retrospect, I was not at all aware of the activities of other revolutionary groups, their experiences and whether they had attempted similar activities. If I had known of their experiences, we could have avoided some common mistakes. And even if we made mistakes, we could have avoided their disastrous consequences and prevented secrets from leaking out. We would not have found ourselves in this situation. I was responsible for the organization and planning, and I could not see any weaknesses. Neither could anyone else who was part of the group. It was as if we were sitting ducks, our eyes closed to the serious weakness in our plans. There were treacherous people too in our midst, and like snakes their poisonous bit finished us off.

Jinhe hum haar samajhte the gala apna sajane ko,
Vahi ab nag ban baithe hamare kaat khane ko.

Those we considered necklaces adorning us
Turned into snakes around our necks, ready to bite us.

There was intense competition among the young members of the group which would often take the form of intense arguments and fights. When matters came to me, I would try to resolve them in a gentle and calm way, bringing their attention back to the principles of the revolutionary group. At times there were disputes about leadership roles. In one of the units, the members had little confidence in their unit in-charge and expressed as much. There had been mistakes made because of the inexperience of the in-charge. All this greatly disappointed and distressed me, for the desire for power (as a leader) is the most dangerous of all. And when it takes over, it corrupts and destroys any organization. Then people spend time competing with each other, criticizing each other, which creates a hostile atmosphere. When I saw these tendencies among the members, I gathered them all and gave them a piece of my mind. They did regret their actions and decided to work with each other amicably. They had faith in me and they did follow my guidance. Still, much damage had been done and there was factionalism within the group. Even then I did not lose faith in anyone, nor became suspicious of anyone's activities. And I ended up here, as God had willed.

Arrest

The police became extremely vigilant after the Kakori dacoity and began their investigation into it. I saw some new faces in Shahjahanpur and a few specific police officials also met me. The entire town was abuzz with details of the Kakori robbery, wondering who might have carried out such a daring act. The police also stepped up their efforts in the town after discovering a couple of robbed notes here. Many friends cautioned me to be careful of the police. One or two people specifically warned me against an impending arrest. I did not heed their advice. I assumed that even if I was arrested, the police would find no evidence against me and would not be able to hold me. I was too confident of myself, and in this manner considered others' advice unnecessary and even foolish before my own judgement. I even entertained the idea of testing the nation's mood—of how sympathetic they would be to our cause if I was arrested. After all, we are willing to sacrifice our lives for the nation—let us see how committed they are in our support. I also thought of gaining the experience of life in jail. Actually, I was simply exhausted, from all the continuous work and responsibilities. I was also feeling a sense of stupor from the thought of possible murders which future work might involve. I did not pay any attention to what the others were saying.

One night I returned home late (around 11 p.m.) from a friend's place. I met some constables of the secret police on the way. They had been paying particular attention to me. I did not care much, and went home and simply slept. I woke up at four in the morning, completed my toilet and soon heard a heavy noise at my door—the sound was that of a rifle butt against the ground. I understood that the police had arrived. I opened the door and stepped out. A police officer came forward, grabbed my hand and arrested me. I was wearing only an angochha around my waist. The office did not seem afraid of the situation. He asked me to surrender any arms I might have at home.

I informed them that I possessed nothing illegal at home. They were rather decent towards me—I wasn't handcuffed. They searched my house and found a letter which was problematic. I had written three or four letters but was not in time to send them in the day's post. So, I simply kept those with me with the intention of posting them in the next cycle. The police found them in my pocket and one of those would create problems. I was taken to the police kotwali. I met an officer of the secret police there. In our conversation, he disclosed a few details which were known only to me and one other member of our organization. There wasn't a third person among us who could have known this information. I was shocked but still not suspicious of this other person because I trusted him completely. I trusted him as much as I would myself. I was also surprised by the nature of arrests made by the police in Shahjahanpur. Some of the people arrested had no evidence against them, nothing to indicate their involvement in our work. How, then, did the police come to know of them? I had no information about the situation in other locations, where our units existed.

It was only in the jail that I got some little information, that it was likely that similar arrests were made at other places as well. The spate of arrests frightened everyone in the town, including our sympathizers and friends. So much so that they did not even arrange for communicating with us while we were in jail.

Prison

As soon as we reached the prison, the secret police arranged to keep us away from each other to prevent communication. But we still managed to talk to each other a little bit. If we were kept in ordinary cells, then it would been very easy, but we were kept in solitary confinement. The same was done to the others arrested in this case, at other locations. The police is at an advantage when it keeps us isolated from each other—they can question us individually, without us having the opportunity to present a united statement. They question us in many ways—at times threatening us, sometimes indulging in small talk to make us reveal minute details. Those experienced with these techniques simply refuse to meet the police—they are well aware that it will not benefit them in any way and only make the situation worse. Some agree to talk to the police in the hope of getting some news about the case. But what are they likely to get from the police anyway? The police are trained in deceit, and they spend their time doing this to all prisoners. But our youth are not trained to spot this or use it to their advantage.

When we did not receive any news, it made us extremely anxious. We were unable to find out what the police were up to, what decisions we should expect in the future—and the longer the period of going without news, the greater our anxiety. The police, in cahoots with the jail authorities, also ensured the case was not discussed when we met our families. The only conversation permitted was that related to family affairs. The most effective way to deal with this situation was to hire a skilled lawyer who would regularly meet and update you about the case. There were no legal hurdles for the lawyer that prevented him from meeting his client, and the conversations between the accused and their lawyer were confidential. They could not be overheard by anyone else. However, I became aware of the existence of these rules only much later. After my arrest, I did try to contact some lawyers in Shahjahanpur, but they were a cowardly lot who did not dare take up a case against the government.

The captain of the secret police met me. After some small talk, he expressed his desire to make me an approver. In a few days, I received news that Banwari Lal had turned approver—a friend who was afraid of being arrested and had been drawn into the case had met Banwari Lal and convinced him to work for the government. Banwari Lal was very nervous, unsure of how the case would turn against him, and given that there was little hope of any assistance from anyone, he was sure of severe punishment. Perhaps if he had got a lawyer, he would have carried on with some courage and hope. Pandit Harkaran Nath had visited Shahjahanpur and met one of the co-accused in the case, Sri Prem Khanna. Sri Khanna urged him to meet the others including me and Banwari Lal, but he did not. Had Pandit Harkaran Nath arranged to meet us, then, possibly, Banwari Lal would have held on and not turned approver. On that night, the police inspector first met Banwari Lal. Once I had slept off, he was taken out of his cell. I woke up at around five in the morning, and not hearing any sound from Banwari Lal's cell, called out to him. The prisoner on duty informed me that Banwari Lal had given his testimony. My friends had cautioned me that Banwari Lal would be the first to betray me, but I did not comprehend this at all. Practically everyone who knew him had made the same observation about him, and cautioned me against giving him sensitive information or responsibility. But now, what was done was done.

A few days later, the district collector met me. He straight up informed me that I would be hanged. 'If you wish to survive, then turn approver in the case.' I did not respond. Then, the police captain visited me. He said many things and showed me several documents. That gave me some idea of how far they had progressed against us. I tried to feed them false information so that they would be misled and waste time in fruitless investigations, but they already had concrete evidence from an inside source. Why would they believe my made-up stories? Then they made me an offer: If I could give a statement mentioning a connection with Bengal and an association with Bolshevik groups, I would get a much reduced sentence, and after my release they would send me to England. I would also be given a reward of 15,000 rupees. I was laughing within. Finally, the captain of the detective force came to meet me in jail. I refused to come out of my cell to meet him. He walked up to my cell and kept on a monologue for several minutes. But he left, frustrated at getting no response from me.

Then came the identification. The police gathered as many people as they could for identifying me. As was my luck, Sri Ainuddin Sahib was appointed the magistrate for the case, and he did everything in his capacity to help the police. We were not allowed the basic rights as the accused, but the paperwork was always maintained so that appearances of a proper process of inquiry were kept up. He had a sweet tongue. He would meet each accused with great enthusiasm, even respect, giving the impression that he sympathized with them. But actually, he was inflicting severe damage. I have never come across such a deceptive, cunning officer. No one had a chance to complain when the case was in the court. If even someone pointed to a lapse, he would manipulate the situation in such a way that no one would be offended or led to believe that some wrong had been committed. In fact, there were instances when he went to the extent of apologizing to the accused in the court in everyone's presence. But on paper, everything he did went against the accused. We realized this and the extent of this deception only when the case reached the sessions court and we received the summons with arguments.

Banwari Lal was arrested in Rai Bareilly before the case proceedings started in court. I came to know of it only recently. I asked Pandit Harkaran Nath to drop everything and meet Banwari Lal immediately, but he paid no attention to me. I had always been a little suspicious of Banwari Lal and did not consider his behaviour becoming of a revolutionary. He would throw his weight around in the presence of other members of the movement, saying that he was the district in-charge and therefore the others should obey him and serve him. He demanded that the others clean his utensils. He was too fond of the good things in life, and would always carry a comb, mirror and soap with him. I was worried that all this would be our undoing, but he had been the confidant of one of the most important of our members. He had helped Banwari Lal by giving him hundreds of rupees; we too were compelled to offer him a monthly subsistence wage from our funds. But none of that helped our cause, and all that I was afraid of came true. The revolutionary-on-hire was unable to bear the responsibility and gave a statement to the police revealing our activities. Some of our members had met him before his arrest, asking him to give away his arms, but he was too drunk on his authority as the district in-charge, and he did not give them up. Once arrested, his pride and authority vanished into thin air. If he had not revealed our movement's secrets, the official case would have been very weak. It was his statement that cost us all dearly. All of us were imprisoned in the district jail in

Lucknow. Initially, we were kept in separate cells, but were brought together just before the case began.

Fighting the court case required money. But what did the accused have? Where could they get money from? It is hard to imagine how they lived. Most did not have relatives who could fight the case on their behalf. And those who did have relatives, these relatives were busy with their families and children. Who would spend time and money chasing a court case? If we had had good legal representation, then the police case would have been seriously weakened. But we were in Lucknow, an effeminate city, where none of its residents even visited the courts. There was not even a press reporter following the court proceedings so that the public could be kept informed. Once, the *Indian Daily Telegraph* did oblige us. It sent a reporter who managed to accurately report all that transpired in the court. But the police, in connivance with the judge, barred him from the court. There was no reaction from the public. In this hopeless scenario, the police got away with whatever they liked, and the judge too was emboldened. He too did whatever he wanted with us. The accused shouted slogans in the court, 'Down, down!' but nothing changed and there was no hearing. A court hearing is still a distant expectation, for Sri Damodar Swarup Seth was left to rot in the prison by the police. He suffered in prison for nearly a year, and he drastically lost weight, from 100 pounds to a mere sixty-six. There were several instances during his imprisonment when he lost consciousness and was nearly dead. He was unable to eat anything for almost ten months. If he was able to drink a few drops of milk, that would cause severe pain in his stomach. His agony was unbearable to watch. A medical board of three doctors was constituted to examine him. They could not comprehend what his ailment was, so declared that there was nothing wrong with him.

Ever since all the accused in the Kakori conspiracy were put together in jail, they had been demonstrating such shocking behaviour that I was quite aghast. The biggest problem was that everyone became a self-styled leader. They showed little consideration for seniority or experience and paid no heed to the advice of those with experience. There was no discipline. They would talk back rudely, and there was constant disagreement, even on the smallest of things. These disagreements would take the form of enmity, and fights broke out among the group members. Well, pots and pans kept together will of course make some noise, and these were humans after all. But it was the one-upmanship and self-styled *netagiri* which really doomed the movement.

The young men who would follow their elders' instructions to the word were now treating them with contempt. The arguments would frequently turn heated and bitter. And regional loyalties came to the fore. The revolutionaries from Bengal and the United Provinces criticized each other. There is no doubt that Bengal has contributed the most to the revolutionary movement, but Bengalis have a strong tendency of promoting regional interests. So much so that if one Bengali joins an office or institution, in a few days' time we will see only Bengalis everywhere in that office. If the Bengali community is present in a town, they will have their own locality dominated by Bengalis. Their language is different. So is their food. These traits were all too evident even in jail. Even those whose selflessness I admired, they too demonstrated a strange commitment to Bengaliness. It was beyond my imagination that members of a revolutionary movement could be so strongly attached to regional loyalties. I was under the impression that the revolutionaries were committed to the liberation of the whole country. What did they care about belonging to a specific region? But as could be seen even in jail, a Bengali's mind was only filled with the poet Rabindranath's song '*Amar Sonar Bangla, Ami Tomay Bhalobashi*' (Oh My Golden Bengal, I Love You), and that sentiment became evident in every little thing they did in their daily lives. I do think it would not have been possible for me to learn of something like this outside jail. Even in the most distressing and agonizing situations, I never let out even a sigh; no tears fell from my eyes at the death of my brother. Yet, there were some members of the organization whom I respected so much that I would get very upset and even cry hearing their harsh words. I could not bear it if they looked at me sternly. My friends, had they seen me in such a state, would have been very surprised at my sensitivity. Now, it was these very venerable people who were creating divisions based on who was Bengali and who was not— my pen shakes as I write these words. They were so blinded by their Bengali sentiment that they could not see the gravest mistakes, stubbornness and cowardice of their fellow Bengalis. Everything done by them was tolerated. This only provided free rein to the plotting and scheming— each day was filled with new schemes of bringing the others down. I was heartbroken at witnessing the state of our revolutionaries. Their behaviour drove me into a depressive state, so much so that I once even considered collaborating with the government.

The barrister sahib initiated a conversation with the police captain. But I dropped the idea, considering the negative impact it would have on the revolutionary group. The group of youth workers in the jail arrived at a consensus that they would go on a hunger strike— we could at least try to improve our conditions while in prison; after all, it was likely we would get very long sentences. It is no mean feat to come out alive after spending time and eating the food in the jails of the United Provinces. Of the many political prisoners kept imprisoned in these jails, at least five or six died due to the harsh conditions and the ill treatment received.

With this in mind, nearly all the accused in the Kakori case began a hunger strike. The next day we were separated from each other. Some were kept in the district jail, others in the central jail. It was only after fifteen days of the hunger strike that the government began to pay attention. It was not that the government was losing anything. Judge sahib and the court officials were earning their salaries sitting at home. The government was more interested in breaking the strike. The jail officials first offered me 8 annas per day. I rejected that offer and with some hard negotiations managed to get that figure raised to 10 annas per day. During the hunger strike I survived only on water. On the sixteenth day I was fed milk through the nose. Sri Roshan Singh-ji also similarly fasted with me for fifteen days, and kept walking and talking all those days. He would even conduct his daily ablutions and toilet. In my case, another person would not have been able to guess, even after ten days, that I had not eaten food.

One of the self-styled leaders would talk to the officials of the secret police formally (in secret) and also informally, when their negotiations were over. I did not pay much attention to them. I did get to hear from here and there that these conversations involved much more than the accused turning approver. Once, I also expressed the desire to meet the chief of the Central Investigation Department (CID), because the police were extremely unhappy with me. But the police prevented any meeting with him, and as result, even the CID became hostile to me. This 'leader' seemed more hopeful (of his release) after his conversations with the officials. As a result, he showed little enthusiasm for the trial and the need to struggle for the release for everyone else involved in the case.

Not only this, misleading information about me was planted to damage my reputation among the young members. The self-styled leader himself spread rumours about me having misappropriated the organization's funds. I had kept accounts of every rupee. As soon as I heard things, I gathered the working committee members, presented a detailed account of all expenses and demanded a punishment for those who were deliberately spreading misinformation against me. The Bengali faction could not tolerate this. Not only were they unwilling to listen to my version of events, they questioned my behaviour and integrity.

The day I finished speaking in my defence, the government-appointed lawyer stood from his place and wholeheartedly praised my speech. He said it was better than those by hundreds of lawyers whom he had heard in his lifetime. I joined my hands in acknowledgement and said that I had no prior experience of spending time in courts. I had found some encouragement once I heard the government and defence lawyers arguing in court.

Following this, the lawyer representing the government started presenting his case against the self-styled revolutionary leader. The case was heavily loaded against the leader, and he grew extremely anxious as the proceedings carried on. He had expected that he might be let off with a relatively lighter sentence, perhaps a maximum of five to ten years' imprisonment in the absence of evidence. But the tide was turning against him. Back in the prison, he met the CID officials for nearly one and a half hours. The youth brigade came to know of this and approached me asking about this meeting. When I inquired, I was told that they were discussing the conditions in which he was to be kept in jail once the sentence was declared. I was not satisfied with this response. After a couple of days, I found the 'leader' sitting alone for a great number of hours, filling several pages with writing. He left these written pages in his clothes' pockets and went away to take his meal. An inner voice told me, 'Get up and see what is going on.' I took out the pages from his pockets and read them with increasing shock and sorrow. It was an apology to the government—he had stated that he would not participate in any violent activity or movement in the future. It was an undertaking too. I questioned some of the main people of the movement, asking them the reason for this apology letter and whether it was no longer necessary to discuss these things within the organization. 'It was a private matter,' I was told. I strongly opposed this attitude and gave them a piece of my mind. This was not a private matter at all. My views caused much sensation among the group and unsettled them. I was furious at their deceit and cunning. It was they who pushed me to fight from the forefront, and they turned out to be the very people conniving against me, accusing me falsely. They boasted of themselves as leaders and gathered young men around them. But when it came to taking responsibility for these twenty-year-olds, when faced with even the smallest of difficulties, these self-styled leaders left them to serve harsh sentences and began writing apology letters to save their own skin. Shame on such a life. However, I kept these thoughts to myself.

The Trial

A special police force was deployed to investigate the looting of the train at Kakori. One Mister Horton was the director of this department. After looking at the site of the robbery and the initial reports of the railway police, he suspected it to be the work of revolutionaries. He turned his attention to the revolutionaries in the state and began investigating them. Three notes of the looted currency were found in Shahjahanpur. A total of more than 100 currency notes, valued at about 1000 rupees, were taken from the train. Out of these, notes worth around 700–800 rupees had already reached the government treasury before the list of stolen notes was released. So the government did not pursue the recovery of the notes and the publication of the list did not help very much. Some of the notes which were found circulating among the public had come out of the treasury itself before the list was released.

Around the same time, the secret police of the district became aware that I was away from Shahjahanpur on 8, 9 and 10 August 1925. They focused their inquiries on me. They found that I had received correspondence related to revolutionary activities through Indubhushan Mitra, a student at the Government School, Shahjahanpur. The letters would reach his address, and he would give them to me. The school's headmaster started making a copy of these letters and sending those to Horton sahib. It was through these copied letters that he came to know of the planned meeting of the revolutionary society of the state in Meerut. Horton sent a sub-inspector to the orphanage which was the pre-decided meeting spot. Similarly, he received information about the planned dacoity in Kankhal and the possible looting of a major post office by the revolutionaries. Horton sahib also got hold of a letter written by me, which mentioned the date 13 September. I had written that my grandfather's *shraad* was on 13 September and invited the addressee to attend it. I said, 'I will see you at the orphanage.' The letter was signed 'Rudra'.

As a preventive measure against the planned dacoities, Horton sahib arrested nearly thirty people from all over the province on 26 September 1925. Around the same time, they got to know from one of the letters received through Indubhushan that some of our belongings, possibly weapons, were stored in a student's room in Banaras. A brief search recovered two rifles from a student's room in the Hindu University. That student was arrested in Kanpur. Indubhushan sent the news of my arrest to Banaras, but the person he sent the letter to, Sri Ramnath Pandey, had already been arrested. A letter addressed to Ramnath Pandey, with his address mentioned, had been found in my possession during my arrest.

The police now possessed all the correspondence. Indubhushan, too, was arrested; the next day, he became a witness. Banwari Lal, who was in Shahjahanpur Jail, met a few co-accused in the jail itself and turned approver. He knew all the key details of the revolutionary society's working and became the prime witness for the government. His statement led the police to the parcels sent by the revolutionaries, and all those who had received them from the Baranas post office were arrested. Gopi Nath, of Kanpur, who too had received the parcel, was arrested, and he immediately became a police witness, giving a statement against his comrades. He also received money orders on behalf of Banwari Lal. Gopi Nath led the police to a relative of Banwari Lal who had kept the latter's belongings. The police found a cartridge pistol, an army revolver and some cartridges. Subsequently, Banwari Lal was arrested. Just in a few days' time he turned approver and government witness in the case—it took only a visit from the police and some sweet-talking by them. This man categorically stated that he had participated in the Kakori dacoity. Over in Dakshineshwar, Calcutta, the police found a bomb, materials to make bombs, seven revolvers and pistols and some seditious literature. From here, they arrested Sri Rajendranath Lahiri, BA, who had been on the run after the Kakori episode.

After Indubhushan's arrest, his headmaster received a letter from the Central Provinces which he redirected straight to Horton sahib. This letter gave away the address of one Mohanlal Khatri of Chanda. Following this lead, the police arrested Sri Ram Kumar Khatri from Poona and sent him to Lucknow. Sri Sachichandra Sanyal was also sent to the Lucknow jail in the Kakori case. He was already serving a lifetime imprisonment term at Kala Pani for the Banaras conspiracy and had been awarded a two-year sentence for distributing revolutionary pamphlets at Bankura. Sri Yogeshchandra Chatterjee, imprisoned in the ordinance case, was transferred from the Hazaribagh jail to Lucknow. He had been arrested in Calcutta after two documents with details of revolutionary committees in the United Provinces and their working in twenty-two districts were found in his possession. The police considered these items as evidence in the Kakori case. Sri Rajendranath Lahiri, who had faced ten years in exile in the Dakshineshwar bomb case, was also sent to Lucknow in the Kakori case. About thirty-six people were arrested. Out of these, twenty-eight were tried in the magistrate's court. Three remained on the run: Sri Sachichandra Bakshi, Sri Chandrashekhar Azad and Sri Ashfaqullah Khan. The remaining were released before the legal proceedings started in court. For two out of twenty-eight, the magistrate let go of the cases. Two were pardoned for becoming approvers. In all, twenty-one accused were tried in the sessions court. By this time, Sri Damodar Swarup was so ill that he could not appear in court. So twenty people remained. From this group, Sri Sachichandra Nath Biswas and Sri Hargovind were acquitted from the sessions court. The remaining eighteen were found guilty.

Mister Banwari Lal was now a government witness. He had once been the minister of the Rai Bareilly District Congress Committee, and he had served six months in prison for participating in the Non-Cooperation Movement. Still, a few threats from the police made him give in. He was the one person in our revolutionary society on whom we spent the maximum amount of money. Even during the most severe fund crunch, he was sent a decent monthly subsistence amount. We did not have enough food to eat, but he was still provided with money. Even then, he did not hesitate before betraying his comrades. What was the maximum punishment he would have received (if he hadn't turned approver)? Ten years? The evidence against him was about the same as that for the other accused, who received ten years' imprisonment. Not only did he expose our workings, he gave them added information which made things worse for us. For instance, he said that Ramprasad spent the loot money on his family. My reaction upon hearing this was one of bitter amusement. This was a person for whose comfort I'd risked my life, for whom I had faced danger and had been badly beaten up, and for whom I did not even pay attention to my parents' well-being— he was the one saying that I had used the money to provide for my family. This was deeply hurtful.

This was the behaviour of the fellow revolutionaries in the organization. Those who were friends, acquaintances from the regular life, exhibited an equally deplorable conduct. One Thakur sahib was arrested for possessing a looted currency note. He must have chanced upon it or received it somewhere in the town. His bail application was rejected and the magistrate asked for a deposit of 4000 rupees. They found no one willing to stand surety for him. His elder brother came begging to me for help, bowed his head at my feet. I tried to arrange for his bail. My parents cautioned me that the police were already hostile and I should avoid openly mobilizing support for him. Still, I did not hesitate in helping him. I went to the court, submitted the bail bonds and then went to the jail to ensure his release. I listed his name as one of my witnesses. But after just slight pressure from the police, he gave it in writing—three separate times—that he did not even know me. The ones whose homes and children I had protected during the Hindu–Muslim communal violence in our neighbourhood turned out to be the very people who gave false statements against me. I was confident that some close friends would unhesitatingly give statements to support my case. Nothing in this world, I believed, would deter them from standing by me. But again, a small conversation with the police and they went back on their promises and refused to testify. The very people whom I considered part of my own self and for whom I readily extended a helping hand and whom I served with the utmost commitment—none of them bothered to even visit me in jail, to say a few words of comfort and support while I was on death row. One or two did oblige me by gathering the courage to make a brief appearance in court and watch the proceedings from a distance. Everyone was terrorized by the police. So it is perhaps understandable, and I can only express my gratitude for whatever anyone could do for me.

Wah phool chadhate hain, turbat bhi dabi jaati
Mashook ke thode se bhi ehsaan bahut hain.

My grave is weighed down by the flowers offered by her.
Even the slightest favours of the beloved are a bounty.

I only pray to God that they all be happy and content. I was well aware of the perils of the path chosen by me. I think I knew little about the workings of the world before this case. I had neither seen a jail nor had I any experience of the judicial process. I learnt much during my imprisonment—it was like a whole new and strange world. I never knew that analysis of handwriting was a branch of study and there were experts who specialized in identifying writers on the basis of writing samples. I did not know that it was possible to compare handwritings, the secrets hidden in one's writing, differences between the writing of two different people, that the experts can track signatures to their writers and know when one person's handwriting style has been copied by another writer. Despite having little experience and knowledge of these intricacies, I was leading the revolutionary society in one province and bearing all its responsibilities. There was no school for training people in revolutionary activities. The only thing possible was that we learn from the experiences of other revolutionaries. There had been so much revolutionary work in Bengal and Punjab, and many had been arrested there. But no one wrote a primer on what to do and what not to do.

The general public must be anxious and wondering: Are the police blessed with great luck that they managed to gather all the information and make a watertight case, or are they all-knowing? How do they become aware of secret activities? I can only lament that this is the nation's misfortune and a blessing for the government. I cannot say much about the Bengali police, because I haven't had much interaction with them. But in the United Provinces, the police are complete idiots who have little common sense. The policemen in regular service enter the secret service. The regular police are involved in patrolling and get fat on bribes. They cannot be bothered to make any effort. The few among them who might be better brains too end up the same—they run after plush and lucrative posts, and once they get those, they have little desire to do a good job. There is no organized secret police in this province who get regular training; they just learn whatever little they do on the job. I realized after the Mainpuri and Kakori cases that if we had been a little more ingenious, it would have been impossible for the police to trace us. In fact, the police did get lucky in the Kakori case. It identified a few people it considered suspicious, met them, had brief conversations with some, threatened a couple of them. And true to the popular saying '*chor ki dadhi mein tinka*', one person instantly threw up all the secrets. All of us were puzzled: how did the police get to know all the details and that too so quickly? We never even considered the gentleman who betrayed us to be the source. But this proved to be true from the conversations I had with the police after my arrest. The police knew exactly the things which only two people in the organization were privy to—me and the said person. The things he did not know remained unknown to the police as well. This was unambiguous proof that it was he who betrayed us. The police would have given up in frustration if he had not been caught and revealed everything to them. The government is wary of proceeding against the accused in even the most outrageous cases, because it does not wish to provoke a mass public protest. It is answerable for its actions. At the most, two to four would have been arrested and they would have been compelled to release them too. Now, the police have clear, direct evidence given by him. Whatever happened, it is God's will and may God bless all. All my life my guiding principle has remained thus:

Sataye tujhko jo koi bewafa 'Bismil'
Toh muhn se kuchh na kehna, aah kar lena
Hum shaheedane wafa ka deen-o-iman aur hai
Sijde karte hain hamesha paanv par jallad ke.

The treacherous may torment you, Bismil.
Speak no words of complaint, give in with a sigh.
We are martyrs to our promise, our
commitment goes beyond,
Our heads bow down forever, at the feet
of our executioners.

I was involved in this case, and the one person whose life I was responsible for was Sri Ashfaqullah Khan Warsi. In these last days of my life, it is my duty to pen down my thoughts and dedicate a few words to him.

Ashfaq

I remember that I met you for the first time when I returned to Shahjahanpur after the imperial declaration. You were very keen to meet me and discuss the Mainpuri case. But I was wary of a Muslim school student wanting to talk to me, and I rebuffed you. You were disappointed and the hurt clearly showed on your face. But you did not give up hope and persisted in your attempts to interact with me. You tried again somehow to have a discussion during the Congress. You tried to convince me of your sincerity and genuine desire to serve the nation, and even got your friends to convey this to me. In the end, you won. You succeeded in winning a place in my heart. I was also pleased to know that your elder brother was my classmate and friend in Urdu middle school. Our bond grew, and soon you were like a younger brother to me. But this did not satisfy you. You wanted to be treated as an equal, as a friend and confidant. And you did become a dear friend to me. Our friendship—between a strict, orthodox Arya Samaji and a Muslim—surprised everyone. I performed the *shuddhi* ceremony for

Muslims, lived in the Arya Samaj mandir, but none of this bothered you. Some of my friends would look at you with contempt and hate for being a Muslim, but this did not prevent you from interacting with me. You would regularly visit me in the Arya Samaj mandir. You were abused by all, called a kafir when Hindu–Muslim communal tensions broke out, but you did not agree with their hate-filled views. You always stood for Hindu–Muslim unity, and you always remained a true Muslim and a true patriot. You would often say that Khuda may bestow some sense upon the Muslims so that the community would work with the Hindus for the greater good of Hindustan. Whenever you saw me writing something in Hindi, you would ask me to write it in Urdu as well so that Muslims too could read it. You learnt Hindi so that you could better understand nationalist feelings. Often, you would end up using Hindi words in your conversations with your family members—something which would surprise everyone.

Many people around you who observed your behaviour were worried that you might give up Islam and undergo shuddhi. But there was nothing impure in your being. What purpose would a purification ceremony serve? Sometimes friends would caution me that I should not trust a Muslim. But your character and integrity completely won me over, so much so that there ceased to be any difference between us. We ate from the same plate. And any ideas I might have had about the differences between Hindus and Muslims simply left me. You have unwavering trust and love for me. Yes, you could not address me by my name. You always called me 'Ram'! This one instance, you were losing consciousness after suffering from heart palpitations. The only sound that escaped from your lips was 'Ram'. All you could utter in this state was 'Ram, Ram'. Those standing near you were aghast. They said you should say Allah's name, but you only said 'Ram, Ram'. Just then a friend who knew what your 'Ram' meant appeared on the scene, and he called for me. Your palpitations and anxiety reduced once I was with you, and the onlookers now understood the meaning of your utterances.

What did this friendship, love and trust lead to? You became completely one with me. You too became a die-hard revolutionary. And all days and nights you were consumed with the goal of imbuing revolutionary spirit in the Muslim youth. You wanted them to contribute to the revolutionary movement, and you tried to mobilize your friends to the cause. Many existing members of the group were apprehensive and surprised that I'd made you, a Muslim, a vital part of the organization. But your work is admirable, and you have never disobeyed or ignored my directions. You were like a dedicated *bhakt* who would readily follow my guidance. You were large-hearted, generous and with impeccable ideals.

I feel immense contentment and pride in you. Your participation in the revolutionary movement will find pride of place in the history of the Indian nation. You paid little heed to the advice of your family and friends, and did not waver in your ideals even after being arrested. You were strongly built, in mind, body and character. As a result of these qualities, you were declared my accomplice and my lieutenant in the Kakori case and were rewarded with the garland of death around your neck (death by hanging). My dear brother, I hope you will be at peace to know that I, who is responsible for your fate, did not hesitate to sacrifice my family's savings (turning them into paupers), my brother's life and my own life for the nation. You may say that I offered my dearest friend Ashfaq to the motherland.

'Asghar' hareem-i-ishq mein hasti hi jurm hai
Rakhna kabhi na paon yahan sir liye hue.

In the sacred space of love, 'Asghar', existence is a crime.
Never put your feet here while bearing your ego high.

Death-Row Cell

My end is near. Two hangings are about to take place. The police have been severely criticized in the newspapers, magazines and among the public at large. In court, I have exposed the judges, the secret police, the magistrate and the government lawyers. My words have made them angry and resentful. I do not have a friend or companion whom I may lean upon in these difficult times; only God keeps me company. These lines from the Gita lend me peace:

Jo kuchh kiya so tai kiya main kachu kinha nahi
Jahan kahin kuchh main kiya tum hi they mujh nahi.

Whatever was done, you did it; I did nothing.
Wherever I did, it was you within me.

Brahmaṇyādhāya karmāṇi saṅgaṁ tyaktvā karoti yaḥ
lipyate na sa pāpena padma-patram ivāmbhasā.

—Bhagavad Gita, 5/16

'Those who perform their duty to the world, without the expectation of any benefit, will be free of sin. Just as a lotus leaf remains untouched by water even when surrounded by it.'

Whatever I have done in my lifetime, it was with the commitment to serve the nation. If I took care to nourish my body, it was with the belief that a healthy, strong body will be of better use to the nation. So, it is after a long *tapasya* that I will see this day [of meeting my death]. This unworthy body is fortunate that it will be offered to the motherland, the first one from the United Provinces after the revolutionary sacrifices during the uprising of 1857.

The government intends to keep me in agony till I meet my end. That is why the date of my execution is fixed in the summer month of April, three and a half months from now. It is like being roasted—spending three and a half months in the death-row cell. It is a tiny space, worse than a birdcage, built in the middle of an open field. It gets no shadow of a tree or building. The sun beats down mercilessly on this room, from eight in the morning till eight in the night, and the sandy ground becomes extremely hot. It is as if raining fire. One side of the cell is a window which is 9 feet wide and 9 feet in length. I eat, excrete, bathe, sleep in this very cell. The mosquitoes keep you entertained through the night. About three to four hours of sleep is all I can manage in the night, that too with much effort. On bad days, it is only one or two hours. The food is served in earthen utensils, and there are two blankets. A life of self-discipline and meditation (tapasya). All the tools necessary for it are available here. Each moment here motivates me to discipline myself, to think of God and prepare myself for the end.

I am in a blissful state in this cell. I had always desired living in an ascetic's cave and practising yoga. This wish has been fulfilled towards the end of my life. This may not be a sadhu's cave, but it is for sure a cave for *sadhana*. The time I spent in this cell gave me an opportunity to write about my experiences and dedicate them to the fellow countrymen. Perhaps the lessons from my life would prove beneficial to another soul. This blessed opportunity has come to me after great hardship.

Mehsoos ho rahe hain baad-e-fanaa ke jhonke
Khulne lage hain mujh pe asrar zindagi ke.

As the gusts of annihilation bear upon me
The secrets of life are now revealed to me.

Baare alam uthaya rang-e-nishat dekha
Aaye nahi hain yun hi andaaz behisi ke.

They experienced the burden of sorrow
and the colours of joy,
Such indifference did not come easily.

Wafa par dil ko sadke jaan ko nazar-e-jafa kar de

Mohabbat mein yeh lazim hai ki jo kuchh ho fida kar de

Now my only desire is

Bahe bahere fanaa mein jalva ya rab luash 'Bismil' ki

Ki bhookhi machhliyaan hain jauhar-e-shamshir katil thi

Samajh kar phoonkna isko zara-e-dagh-e-nakami

Bahut se ghar bhi hain aabad is ujade hue dil se.

Let the heart be sacrificed for loyalty and the soul be
sacrificed for betrayal.

In love, it is essential to sacrifice everything,
whatever you have.

O God, let the body of 'Bismil' float in the
ocean of mortality.

The killer's skill with the sword is like ravenous fish.

Take care before you extinguish this heart, it bears
marks of failure,

Yet many homes are flourishing from this
desolate heart.

The Results

What were the results of our unceasing commitment
and efforts of the past eleven years? This might not

be a worthwhile question to ask, for the simple reason that we did not become part of the revolutionary movement with the calculation of any profit and loss, or victory and defeat. We did what we did with a sense of sincere duty. What would be worthwhile is an evaluation of how intelligently and effectively we could carry out our duties. Politically, our movement only succeeded in aggravating the difficulties of the youths who joined us, some of them losing their lives in vain. We spent money too.

According to the Hindu shastras, no one meets an untimely death; people die as per what is written in their fate. Their end is decided by fate; it is just that the conditions for it appear in this world. Lakhs of people in this country die of epidemics, cholera and plague. Many more die in famines. Who is responsible for them?

As for the money we spent, a far greater amount is spent by people in celebrating marriages. Our expenses for executing a single plan would not be greater that what the elite men in the town spend on leisurely activities in a month. We were the ones labelled dacoits, and punished with death and Kala Pani. But, in our view, it is the lawyers and doctors who are actually looting people. They are the greater dacoits. These lawyers and doctors swallow entire properties of even the most influential *talukdar*s. In Awadh, the mansions built by lawyers mock the trapped and helpless talukdars. In Lucknow, the doctors have their own palaces. But these men who rob in plain sight are considered distinguished and respectable. What is the difference between these daytime robbers and the dacoits who raid at night? Both take away other people's money for their self-interest.

The revolutionary movement's contribution is historically significant. There is no doubt that the Indian youth has aspirations of freedom, even if in a nascent stage. Even with their limited capacity they initiate steps to achieve it. If the situation had been more favourable, these few young men would have startled the world with their work. And then, the Indian youth too would have had the opportunity to proclaim—as was proclaimed by the French revolutionary youth after the establishment of the Republic—that the monuments of independence which have been built so far should serve as a lesson to the oppressors and as an inspiration for the oppressed.

There were just twenty-one men accompanying Ghazi Mustafa Kemal Pasha when he left Turkey. He had no possessions, just a death warrant which chased him. But events turned rapidly, and the same Kemal left the world awestruck with his wondrous deeds. Kemal Pasha, once hounded as a murderer, was now hailed as the architect of Turkey. The great (mahatma) Lenin once made a narrow escape to save his life by hiding in barrels of wine. The same Mahatma Lenin shaped the future of Russia. Sri Shivaji, too, was considered a raider and a dacoit. But when his time came, the Hindu community made him their chief, and he was addressed as Chhatrapati (one who bears the royal canopy) and celebrated as the protector of the Gaur Brahmans. So much so that the Government of India had to erect memorials to him to save their own skin. Even Clive was a stubborn, difficult student who had given up in his life. Time changes, so did his fate: he was celebrated as Lord Clive, one of the best-known colonial administrators of British rule in the region. Sri Sun Yat-Sen was a Chinese anarchist, on the run, who went on to become the President of the Republic of China. Success determines a person's life. When success eludes a person, he is labelled cruel, a dacoit, anarchist, traitor and murderer. If he achieves success, he is celebrated as kind, benevolent, just, democratic and great.

There is no doubt that at present, the political, religious and social conditions in the country do not favour a revolutionary movement. Yet, the history of the nation will have to acknowledge us. Indians lack education, and they hesitate to embrace or embark upon even the most ordinary of social reforms. What response can one expect in the field of political change? For a political transformation, we need a revolutionary organization which is built to withstand the distractions and hurdles, which are sure to come in its way. The organization's work should continue despite these difficulties. The organization should have enough capable workers who can stand in for one another should anyone be unavailable.

So many secret revolutionary activities all over India were exposed and their organization ruined. Who will commit to revolutionary work if this is the condition of the revolutionary organizations? Our country's people should be educated so that they can judge the government's policies and their own as good or bad. They should be able to evaluate whether they should rid themselves of this government, and if yes, then devise ways of bringing about that change. What is a revolutionary organization? What does it wish to achieve? These questions and their answers must be taken to the public at large. Only when the common people are sympathetic to the movement will any revolutionary organization be able to plant its feet in the country. These are just initial thoughts on the formation of a revolutionary group. The revolution is yet far.

The mere thought of a revolution is scary for people. Any transformation will be opposed by those who benefit from the status quo. For instance, daybreak is uncomfortable for nocturnal beings. Birds and animals used to cold weather migrate when the temperatures get warm. Political transformations will, of course, be terrifying. Human beings are, after all, creatures of habit. Habits internalized over a period of time shape our nature and behaviour. Anything which stands in opposition or variation to our habits is therefore scary. Moreover, every ruling dispensation has its supporters—the rich and landed zamindars. These elites will never favour any change which disrupts their comfortable life, and that is why they always work to destroy the revolutionary movement. Even if there is a revolution in the country, whether with the help of another country or if the conditions are ripe, then too the lack of an able leadership will turn the situation into an anarchy. In such a case, lives are needlessly lost, and this whole process simply destroys brave fighters and intellectuals. The most striking example of this is the revolt of 1857.

Even if we are successful in overthrowing the monarchy and establishing a republic, as was done in America and France, it will be the rich men who will capture all the rights and privileges by virtue of their power and influence. In working committees, they would end up with all the authority. In governance, their views would be given the most importance. With money, they control the newspapers, industries and the mines/natural resources. The majority of the public just ends up supporting this elite. When they get an opportunity, some clever people who are part of the intelligentsia do not hesitate to deprive the common people of their rights. Their selfish interests do not allow them to promote the interests of the working class and the farmers. As a result, they end up building a system where money rules (plutocracy). This was what happened after the Russian Revolution, and the revolutionaries there had anticipated this. They first overthrew the monarchy and then, as soon as the moneyed class and the intelligentsia tried to make use of this opportunity, the revolutionaries fought them off to establish a democracy.

Let us consider this. What are the resources and conditions in our country which support the revolutionary movement? In the previous pages, I have already shared that we struggled to provide two meals to the members of our organization. It was through tireless efforts, after the Non-Cooperation Movement ended, that we managed to get a few young men in the United Provinces to support us. Out of these few, there were even fewer who truly believed in revolutionary work and had the courage to give up their lives for it. These young people were brought into the revolutionary movement with the promise and hope of change and lofty ideals, that too at a time when the government was extremely hostile (after the Non-Cooperation Movement), and one was readily labelled a traitor. The youngsters who joined were inspired through the possibility of help from the Bolsheviks, and the motivating stories of past revolutionaries and their sacrifices. The youth are naturally attracted to the revolutionary ideals and its heroes; they are also keen to handle arms, use a revolver—all of this makes them sympathetic to the revolutionary movement.

In my own revolutionary life, I haven't come across a single young man who was not impatient to handle a revolver or a pistol. The moment they got hold of one, it was as if they had acquired divine power and thereafter expected half of their life's problems to vanish. They also began to assume that the group must possess a large stock of weapons, for it was preparing to fight the entire government. Therefore the group must also have lots of money. And that next, they would get to travel across the country for revolutionary work (on trips funded by the group), meet great personalities, get inside information on the workings of the secret police and read the literature which had been seized by the government (and was not available here, near home). They also seemed to be under the impression that the revolutionaries had won over the rulers and princes of the country. So now, nothing could stop us from overthrowing this government. We, too, would learn to make a bomb. This was the solution to all our problems, and so on. These young men began to contribute to the society's work, and in some became more involved as active members; that was when they realized their actual position, and understood the serious, dangerous and difficult mission they were involved in. Then they were in the same situation as the members of the 'Nakata Panth'* were in the well-known story.

Failures and treachery from confidants are a feature of the life of a revolutionary, and one can only conclude that these are part and parcel of the difficult path we have chosen. Revolutionaries in other countries too must have faced similar hurdles. One finds solace in inspiring words such as 'the brave do not abandon their chosen path'. Even the educated citizens of the country don't know anything about revolutionary work,

---

* Bismil is referring to a funny folk tale which goes like this: In a village, the panchayat cut off the nose of a person of bad character as punishment. So, 'Nakata' (he whose nose had been cut off) left the village and became a sadhu. One day, a curious man asked, 'Baba, how did your nose get cut?' Nakata replied, 'The nose is a symbol of the ego. It was a hindrance to seeing God, so I had it cut off.' The man also wanted to see God by giving up his nose. The next day, after performing a ritual, Nakata cut off his nose. The man started writhing in pain, and after some time he realized that he could not see God. He asked Nakata, 'Where is God?' Nakata replied, 'When God came, you were writhing; now He is gone.' The man asked, 'What will happen to me now?' Nakata said, 'Now shout that I saw God. I saw Him after getting my nose cut, by the grace of Guruji. Otherwise people will despise you and call you Nakata.' The devotee understood and shouted, 'I saw, I saw God! I saw Him!' People applied tilak on his forehead and made him a Paramhansa. Thus, the Nakata sect was founded.

let alone the masses. How should we expect them to sympathize with us? And without the pressure of public opinion and public support the government does not care very much. There might be a couple of articles in muted words about us in the English newspapers, but they prove entirely ineffective. These words disappear without a trace, without anyone having paid attention to them. After observing and considering all things, I can conclude that I am glad that I did not run away and allowed my arrest. I did have the opportunity and the means to escape. I had been tipped off about my impending arrest; I could have easily disappeared, and the police would have had difficulty tracing my whereabouts. But I was adamant to test myself. Even after the formal arrest, I was walking freely down the street for about half an hour and could have made a run then. Policemen were sitting on the side without a bother in the world. When we reached the kotwali in the afternoon, there too I sat without any handcuffs. A single constable was directed to watch over me, and he was tired after an overnight duty. All the officers had been busy making arrests all over the area—they too had worked all night. They went off to rest. The constable keeping watch over me slid into a deep sleep. A single man, a *munshi* keeping records, remained at the kotwali office. He was a relative of one of the accused, Sri Roshan Singh. If I had wanted, I could have simply walked off. But I realized that if I escaped, the munshi would be blamed for it. I casually remarked to him, 'If you don't mind a little questioning and the following punishment [from the officers], I would like to go.' He, of course, knew me and fell on my feet, begging me not to do so—pleading that he would be arrested, punished and his family and children would die hungry. I took pity on him. An hour later some policemen returned to the kotwali after searching Sri Ashfaqullah Khan's home. They deposited a cartridge gun and a box full of cartridges (belonging to Ashfaq's brother) with the munshi. I was sitting beside him, and there was just a single unarmed constable near me. For an instant, I was tempted to grab the gun and cartridges. Who could stop me, after all? But I immediately dropped the idea because that would have put the munshi in trouble, and I did not wish to betray his trust. Just then, the deputy superintendent of the secret police walked on to the terrace and saw that I was sitting in the office, unrestrained, and there were weapons around me within easy reach. A gun and cartridges were lying on one side of me, and Sri Prem Krishna's Mauser pistol and its cartridges were on the other side. These weapons were deposited with the munshi as part of police routine. He immediately ordered their removal and sent them off for safekeeping in the deposit room. I decided that I should make a run for it now. I stepped out with the excuse of going to the toilet, with a constable accompanying me. Another constable advised him to tie me up, but he replied that he was confident I would not run away. The toilet was located in an isolated spot, and once I entered it, the constable turned away and started watching a wrestling match taking place a little distance away. I climbed the wall and saw that the constable was quite engrossed in the match. With another heave I could have jumped over the wall and made my escape. But it immediately crossed my mind that the constable had trusted me and allowed me freedom of movement. I should not misuse his trust—he might be jailed for this lapse. Would this be a good act on my part? What would his children think of me then? These sentiments prevented me from escaping, and my heart did not permit me to go any further. I took a deep breath, climbed down from the wall back into the toilet, and returned to the kotwali with the constable.

The Kakori accused enjoyed a high degree of freedom in the Lucknow jail. All thanks to Rai Sahib Pandit Champalal, the jailer, it was like enjoying a stay as a guest at a relative's house rather than being imprisoned. We would get upset every now and then about minor things, and make demands of him. But he treated us like his own children, so large-hearted was Pandit Champalal-ji. If any of us were uncomfortable, he would be worried and upset about it. This was his attitude not only towards us but towards all the prisoners and staff, including constables, cleaners and the munshi. As a result, everyone was happy. Moreover, the constables on guard duty in the prison looked upon me with immense respect, as they would upon their guru. This was because they observed my daily routine and self-discipline. I would wake up at three every morning without fail—whether it was hot, cold or rainy—and perform my ablutions, followed by prayers (sandhya) and the havan. I was practically worshipped by every guard on duty. If any member of their family fell ill, they would ask for ash from the havan and carry it back with them; others requested for talismans. Because of their belief in me, they would often feel better—which only deepened their faith in me. So the situation was quite favourable to me, and I had everything in place to make my escape from the prison. I could have left quietly whenever I wished to. One night, I did prepare myself to escape. It was as if the *nambardar*s who guarded the barracks relied upon me. They would intermittently sleep while on duty and banked upon me to save them if they were caught doing so. They were confident that if they were tried before the officers, I would speak on their behalf and save them. The constables, too, did not worry much. All was quiet that night. The only thing I had to be careful about was carrying out the iron chains without making a noise. I had cut the chains four months back and piled them up in such a way that despite daily inspections and regular procedures like washing, painting, dusting and testing their joints by an iron mallet—done in the jail—no one could spot that they had been cut. The moment I stood up to escape as I had intended, I was immediately struck by the thought of Pandit Champalal. He had been kind to us, and I had enjoyed a comfortable stay and freedom in jail thanks to him. Now he was old, towards the end of his career, and his pension would soon be due. How could I hurt him by running away? I had never betrayed anyone in my life and decided that I was not going to do so now. By this time, I was well aware that I would be punished by death; still, with Pandit Champalal in my mind, I decided not to run away. My words might appear to be ramblings of a delirious mind, but all this is true and can be confirmed from evidence.

I have come to the conclusion that if we had directed our efforts towards educating the masses and spreading awareness among them, our actions might have been more successful and more lasting. I believe that it would be more fruitful for the Indian youth to direct their energies in mobilizing the common people of India rather than engage in secret revolutionary work, and in organizing the working class and the farmers into unions to stand against the injustices of the rich and the zamindars. The elites in our country favour the government. The middle class remains dependent on all three—the rich, the zamindars and the government—in one way or another. Their jobs and businesses are courtesy of these ruling elites. And as far as the working class and the farmers are concerned, they spend all their time and energy in trying to keep their stomachs full. Where do they get the time to think about religion, society and politics? They are unable to even maintain appropriate behaviour due to ills like alcoholism. Their lives are clouded by problems like adultery, infanticide, premature deaths and disease. There has been an absence of initiative from the farming class. If a farmer earned 2 annas daily or 4 rupees a month twenty years ago for working for a zamindar or ploughing his land, he is still working on the same wage today. The farmer was on his own, a single person, twenty years ago, but today he has a wife and four children. And he still survives on the same wage. He has to make do with it. He will get night blindness from continuously working in the sugarcane field in the harsh glare of the summer sun, braving hot, searing winds (*loo*). He will be unable to see at night, and for all this labour he will probably get half a ser of *sharbat* (made from fermented molasses) or half a ser of gram and 6 paise of daily wage. He has to keep his family alive on this.

Those who in their hearts desire to serve the country, those who yearn to see their motherland free and independent, should direct their efforts towards organizing rural society, improving the farmers' lot and instilling in them the desire to work for change rather than live by fate alone. Workers' unions must be established in industries, the railways, ships, factories—wherever there is a labouring class—so that workers become aware of their rights and can no longer be exploited by the owners. Education and equal social rights must be a priority for the untouchables, who constitute more than 6 crore of this country's population. Can the citizens of a country claim the right to freedom when the same country considers 6 crore people untouchable? Along with this, women's condition must be improved so that they may at least consider themselves part of human society. At present, their status is not considered above the status of a maid or like a doll in the house. When we see progress in these sections, when we see the majority of our people educated and able to judge right or wrong, then any movement supported by them is sure to succeed. Then even the greatest powers in the world will be unable to crush them. In Russia, until the farmers organized themselves, the government continued to oppress the nationalists. It was only when Catherine took up the responsibility of mobilizing the rural population, established peasant-reform associations at several places and travelled from place to place mobilizing the young men and women in Russia against the Czar that the farmers became aware of their position and could judge good from bad. That was when the foundations of the Czarist regime began to shake. Labourers' unions were formed in Russia, and they began striking for their rights. The strength of public opinion and the masses awakened those who were drunk on power.

In India, our greatest limitation is that the youth have now tasted urban comforts and are addicted to it. They are now used to fancy clothes, walking on paved roads, eating spicy foods, sweets and savouries, spending time in markets filled with gorgeous foreign goods, sitting at a table and using chairs. They remain immersed in a life of comfort and consumption, and are contemptuous towards rural life. According to them, people in villages are primitive, uncultured and uncivilized. If, by any chance, a young student of an English-medium school or college happens to visit his relatives in the village, it becomes impossible for him to spend even a couple of days there. He either carries a novel with him to read or simply sleeps to while away the time. He is either impatient and tired at the prospect of having a conversation with a villager or considers it beneath him to do so. Even the rich villagers, such as the zamindars, who send their sons to English-medium schools, wish for them to get a government job and leave the village. And as soon as these rural youth reach the town, they are so smitten by its attractions, so obsessed with the fashions that they become unrecognizable. It takes only a few days for their character to be affected by all this, and they pick up bad habits by keeping bad company. They can hardly reform themselves. How can one expect them to improve the conditions of India's villages?

The Non-Cooperation Movement saw a large participation, but most workers confined their activities to giving speeches in the cities. There were few who went to the villages, and they too spent their energy in rabble-rousing, as if that was the most important service to the nation. As a result, the movement scattered as soon as it lost momentum. That was why the great Deshbandhu Chittaranjan Das declared that organizing the rural masses was the goal of his life. In my opinion, the most effective way of making such an organization would involve getting the youth to give up their urban lifestyle and develop a connection to rural India. The youth spend several thousand rupees to get middle, entrance, FA, BA degrees, and end up slogging at a job which pays them maybe 10, 20 or 30 rupees. Instead, they could learn skills and set up their own work like carpenters, iron smiths, tailors, washermen, weavers, cobblers, builders, masons, etc. If they would like to maintain hygiene, they could learn medicine. Start your enterprise in a settlement or a large village. If they pursue any of the vocations mentioned above, it is very possible to earn 30 rupees a month with four to five hours of work every day. Thirty rupees in the village is worth 60 rupees in the city. This is because the cost of living in the village is lower—wood and cloth are cheaper. If a zamindar feels generous, he may have a dead tree cut down and let you carry away its wood—that takes care of your fuel for at least six months. Milk and pure ghee are cheaper in the village, and if you keep a cow or a buffalo, it is even easier and better. The fodder is not expensive; the ghee–milk can be consumed by the family, especially children; the dung can be used as fuel. Sometimes people give away one or two cartloads of hay after the crop has been harvested. Most workers in the village do not need to spend money on fodder or wood.

There must be thousands of decent villages which do not have a *vaidya*, a tailor or a washerman, and therefore the residents are compelled to travel long distances, sometimes up to 10–20 *kos*, to avail these services. This is a stressful life. For instance, during weddings it becomes impossible to arrange for clothes. One can prescribe medicines with some ordinary training and by referring to a few basic texts—that should easily bring in an income of 30–40 rupees per month. This is sufficient to sustain oneself even with a family. In villages, it is easier for people to know one another, and not just as mere acquaintances. If you help people even a little bit, they remain grateful forever. You will always be held in respect, and their help will be readily available in your need. There isn't a single person in the village who does not need the services of an iron smith, carpenter, washerman, tailor, potter or doctor. I have seen how simple folk in the village maintain good relations with them.

And these relationships can become the basis for a greater interaction with the villagers—on the ways in which their lives can be transformed.

This can be a fruitful intervention which can make them true khadi-wearing, swadeshi patriots in a short time. Those who can read and write may subscribe to newspapers so that they keep themselves informed of what is happening in the country. They can be encouraged to give up social evils by discussing books and stories. It may be beneficial to organize a public reading of the Ramayana or the Bhagavad Gita once in a while. Such occasions are likely to attract donations, which can be used to establish a public library for the community. And these public readings of the Ramayana or the Bhagavad Gita can easily be interspersed with political discussions—no secret police officer is interested in these gatherings. On the other hand, if a khadi-clad person wants to give a speech in the village, the zamindars immediately alert the police. So, doctors, teachers or priests who lead the public readings of the texts are in a better position to convey political messages, which will be taken more seriously by the common people. Similarly, there can be other ways of making inroads into rural India and improving people's lives. Night-time schools may be opened to teach the children of the poor and the untouchables. A workers' union can be established in the cities, but this also means that one has to spend more time on mobilizing them. One can talk to them only when they return home after a long day's work. They are always short on time. We will have to find more attractive and effective ways of gathering them and spreading awareness among them, such as through magic-lantern shows and night-time schools for them and their children. The young men who plan to waste money on higher education are better advised to study in the English medium till the tenth standard and subsequently learn a vocation. They may make a life through these skills and professions.

Some rich and elite people have established large educational institutions in the service of the nation. They should also consider having schools of vocational training along with these institutions bestowing degrees. And these institutions must be wary of ambitious, self-styled leaders. The students must make 'simple living and high thinking' their motto. Those who truly wish to serve the nation must be willing to bear hardships and work in an organized manner to make a lasting impact, just like Catherine did. Her followers would sew clothes or make shoes to sustain themselves in the villages they would travel to, and use the night time to talk to the villagers on political issues. I was deeply influenced by the biography of Catherine, which I read in English (*The Grandmother of the Russian Revolution*). I immediately translated it into Hindi and got it published as *Catherine*. I would have liked to emulate her but got entangled in revolutionary activities. I am now convinced that no revolutionary organization can be successful in India, even for the next fifty years, as the conditions are not conducive for revolution. That is why it is foolish to attract the country's youth to revolutionary work and ruin their lives in the process. It is likely to do more harm than good. My final message to the youth is that they should choose to serve the nation sincerely instead of entertaining the romantic idea of using revolvers or pistols. Their goal should be total independence, and they should learn to be true communists. God will help them if they selflessly and wholeheartedly dedicate themselves to the nation, rather than hope for rewards.

Yadi desh hit mein marna padhe mukjhko sahashron baar bhi

To bhi na mein is kasht ko nij dhyan mein laaun kabhi

He Ish, Bharat Varsha mein shat baar mera janam ho

Kaaran sadaa hi mrityu ka, deshopakarak karma ho.

I can die a thousand times over in the service

of the nation.

Never once paying attention to the agony I face.

O God, let me take a hundred births in India,

Each death may be in the cause of the nation.

Some Thoughts in the Final Moments

I write these lines on 16 December 1927. The day
when this body will be hanged and this life will end
has been decided: 19 December 1927 (Paush Krishna,
11 Samvat 1984 Bikrami), at six-thirty in the morning.
This *leela*, play, of life will come to an end. It is the
Almighty God's leela; after all, he decides everything.
He alone determines when and how a life will come to
its end. The conditions of death are mere earthly tools.
The shastras have laid down that as long as karma is
not fulfilled, the atma continues to be trapped in the
circle of life and death. Although it is only the Brahma

who will evaluate the karma done by this atma and decide which form it will take in the next birth, I am resolute in my belief that I shall be reborn stronger, with renewed powers, in the home of a relative or a dear friend so that I may continue on my supreme mission of establishing a free and just society (equitable distribution of natural resources for all human beings). People's rule should be established in all parts of the world. India's current situation is most worrisome. It will take many more rebirths in this land till the time the men and women of this country are free in every way. I pray to God to give me birth in this very land so that I might propagate his divine message (Ved Vani) among human beings. It is possible that I might make mistakes in choosing this path, in the decisions I make, but I am not to blame—after all, I am a mere creature. Only the all-knowing God makes no mistakes. We carried out our tasks in the conditions given to us and shall continue to do so. May God bestow me with wisdom to pursue my path and to minimize my errors.

It is now important to note down and share everything that happened to the accused in the Kakori conspiracy case after the sessions court gave its verdict.

The sessions judge pronounced his verdict on 6 April 1927, and an appeal against it was submitted in the Chief Court of Awadh on 18 July 1927. The sentences of most of the accused were increased, and one or two were even reduced. Before the hearing on the appeal, I had submitted a petition to the governor of the United Provinces, in which I pledged not to participate in revolutionary activities in the future. This application was part of my final appeal for mercy, submitted to the judges of the Chief Court. But none of these were entertained by the judges. I had written the arguments for my own case and submitted these to the court. The judges were taken aback by the quality and the strength of my arguments, and did not quite believe that those were penned by me. The overall result was that the court declared me the chief conspirator and most dangerous one. The judges did not believe my pleas of mercy and regret; they expressed their conviction that if released, I would repeat my actions. They noted my sharp mind and labelled me a 'heartless killer'. Well, they wielded the pen and could put down any decision they liked, but to anyone reading the judgment, the reasons for punishing me with death become all too evident. After all, Ramprasad had pointed fingers at the sessions judge, spoken against the secret police, exposed the injustices which happened during the trial. That was why Ramprasad was declared the greatest criminal. And pardon or leniency was not possible, no matter how much he pleaded.

As per the procedure, my mercy petitions were sent to the governor of the province and then to the viceroy after my appeal was rejected in the Chief Court. A petition signed by nearly all the members of the Legislative Council of the United Provinces was also submitted—it asked for the commutation of the death sentence given to Ramprasad Bismil, Rajendra Lahiri, Roshan Singh and Ashfaqullah Khan, into other penalties. My father submitted another petition signed by 250 elites, honorary magistrates and zamindars, but none of these had any effect on the government of Sri Sir William Morris. Yet another letter was sent to the viceroy, signed by seventy-eight members of the Legislative Assembly and the Council of State, stating that the accused in the

Kakori case had expressed regret about their actions and requesting that their sentences be transmuted from the death penalty, as was recommended by the flying squad judges. But the viceroy paid no attention to these.

Pandit Madan Mohan Malviya-ji and some other members of the assembly met the viceroy to convince him to commute the death sentence. After the meeting, we were hopeful that something positive may come out of it. But the government quietly sent telegrams to the prisons two days before Vijaydashmi, saying there was no change in the punishment. The date of hanging was set. The superintendent of the jail read out the telegram to me. My only response was that you should go ahead with your duty. He insisted that I send a mercy petition to the emperor. He told me about the rule whereby any prisoner whose mercy petition had been rejected by the viceroy could still send one to the government, addressed to the emperor of British India. No other superintendent of jail would have suggested so. As I wrote this appeal, I considered submitting an application to the Privy Council in

England. I got in touch with a lawyer in Lucknow, Sri Mohanlal Saxena, and he somehow submitted the appeal in the Privy Council. We already knew what to expect. The appeal was rejected there too. One may ask: even after knowing the hostile attitude of the government, why did I petition it at all? Why did I send one appeal after another, asking for mercy?

As I understand it, politics is like a game of chess. Chess players are well aware that they need to sacrifice some chess pieces for tactical gain. When in the Bengal ordinance case it was proposed in the assembly that the prisoners be released or tried in open court, the government vehemently opposed the idea, arguing that it had impeccable evidence against the accused. An open trial would compromise the safety of the witnesses. The government may consider commuting their sentences if the accused would submit an application pledging that they would not participate in any revolutionary activity. After the Dakshineshwar case and the Shobha Bazaar ordinance case in Bengal, another case was tried in open court— the assassination of the deputy superintendent of the secret police—and so were some other cases where the accused were held on murder charges. But the police were unable to provide any evidence of danger to the witnesses. The Kakori case trial ran for one and a half years in the court. Nearly 300 witnesses were presented by the government. Many informers and eyewitnesses moved around freely while the trial went on—the police could never present any evidence of threat to their lives. I submitted a written bond to the government, exposing their double standards. The government had declared the Bengal ordinance accused to be dangerous conspirators, murderers participating in violent revolutionary activities, and it claimed to have watertight evidence against them. The same was said in the case of the Kakori accused. Why, then, did the government not consider the latter's written pleas? As the saying goes, '*Jabra mare rone na dey*', that is, the bully will beat you up and not even let you cry. I know that all the political trials in the United Provinces are decided on the whims of the secret police. In the Bareilly police constable killing incident, completely innocent young men were falsely implicated in the case and the judgment was written from what was penned down in the diaries of CID officials. The same happened in the Kakori case. My own actions were carried out with the objective of exposing their manipulations and deceitful statements. The government had no valid reason for rejecting the mercy pleas of the Kakori accused. Everything that happened in the Bengal ordinance case was applicable in the Kakori case too. There was absolutely no possibility of the deterioration of law and order or peace if the Kakori accused were spared the death penalty. Especially when all the members of the assembly, Hindus and Muslims, had come together to sign the petition supporting us. There was no precedent of demonstration of such overwhelming support to revolutionaries. But the government did not wish to show any leniency in this case. It remained arrogant, proud of its brute strength. There was clear evidence that the accused in the Hindu–Muslim communal riots in Shahjahanpur and Allahabad had killed people in broad daylight. But their death sentences, which had been awarded by the Allahabad High Court, were commuted by Sir William Morris. And at a time when there were increasing instances of communal violence. So, if according to the government, letting the Kakori accused live would encourage other revolutionary groups to emulate them, then surely this logic is applicable to the communal violence cases too. Clearly, the government's intent is different. They wish to keep India under their subjugation. Even the most moderate leaders do not find a place in the commissions set up by the imperial authorities; the speeches of the Secretary of State Lord Birkenhead and those by the leaders of the Labour Party have made it evident that the government is only set to tighten the chains that enslave India.

I do not think that we give our lives in vain. I believe that our deep, collective sighs of pain and our desire to be free scared Lord Birkenhead into fuelling Hindu–Muslim divisions and profiting from it, and thereby strengthening colonial rule in India. But as the saying goes, '*Gaye the namaz chhudane, roze gale pade*', that is, the British hope to gain from dividing us, but they only ended up uniting us. Across India, leaders of all major political parties, which include most Hindus and the majority of Muslims, have in one voice strongly protested the commission and its members. The Hindus and Muslims stand united, and the members of different political groups are coming together as the next Congress session in Madras approaches. When our mercy petition was rejected by the viceroy, I immediate wrote a letter to Sri Mohanlal-ji saying that Indian nationalist leaders and the Hindu–Muslim groups should remember and celebrate us at the Madras Congress. The government declared Ashfaqullah Khan as the right-hand man of Ramprasad. If a staunch Muslim, Ashfaq, can be the right-hand man of Ramprasad, a staunch Arya Samaji, is it not possible for Hindus and Muslims of the country to forget their petty differences and unite for India's freedom?

God has accepted my prayers, and I can see my wish coming true. My work is done. I have presented Ashfaq, a young man from the Muslim community, to all Indians. He has proven himself. No one should now dare to claim that Muslims cannot be trusted. Ashfaq was the first example and a complete success. I plead to my fellow countrymen that if our deaths meant anything to you, if they made you even a little sad, then the Hindus and Muslims and the different political groups should unite under the banner of the Congress. Follow the guidance of the Congress. If this happens, then the day is not far when the British government will be compelled to bow down to our demands and our independence will be within reach. No matter how fraught the process, the unity of Hindus and Muslims will enable us, help us and is our greatest desire. Ashfaq is with me on this; what I write here is his opinion too. Our death-row cells in the Lucknow Jail were next to each other while the appeal was pending. We spent several days together, talking to each other about various things. After our arrests, Ashfaq was desperate that he should meet me at least once; God fulfilled his desire.

Sri Ashfaqullah Khan was vehemently against filing the mercy petitions. His unwavering belief was that Allah was the only one before whom one should pray for mercy and the only one who could grant pardon. But he relented upon my insistence. I am the one guilty of using his love for me, of making him give up his decision. I wrote to him from the Gorakhpur Jail, on the occasion of Bhratri Divitiya (Bhai Dooj), begging for his forgiveness for my actions. God only knows if he received that letter. Well, it was God's will that we are to be hanged; our deaths will be like salt on the wounds of our fellow countrymen and they will cry out in agony, and may our souls be at peace upon watching their future actions. When we are reborn in this country, ready and eager to serve it, India may be liberated politically, its masses living in safety and peace, and rural India may reach an improved state, with its people realizing their duty.

There was a purpose behind spending time and money on the appeal to the Privy Council. All the appeals were meant to drive home the point that the death penalty is not justified. It is still not known who shot the man who died. If the death penalty was awarded for carrying out the dacoity, then according to the observations of the Chief Court, I was the leader of the group and its activities in the province, and I led the looting. So I alone should be punished by death and not the other three. They should be given other punishments. But why would the government allow this to happen? This was a test for these foreign courts and leaves us Indians with the lesson that we should not trust these English courts in political cases. And if required, we should give unrestrained, fearless statements at the proceedings. Otherwise, my position remains that one should not make the mistake of appearing before these courts or presenting statements in them.

What happened in the Kakori case proceedings is a lesson for all of us. The case shows us all that could possibly be wrong and unjust. Another reason why I wrote to the Privy Council was that I wanted to delay the final punishment, to see how the youth of the country are moved by this whole case and how my fellow countrymen can help. I was most disappointed by their response, enough to think of planning an escape from the jail. Had I done so, the government would have been forced to commute the death sentences of the other three, and if not on their own, I would have found ways to compel them to take this decision. I made several escape attempts but received no help from outside the jail. It is deeply hurtful that I could not even find a revolver from an outside source to defend myself after my escape—in a place where I built and led such an impressive revolutionary organization. No young man came forward to help me. In the end, I await my hanging. I am not distressed by the prospect of my death, for it was God's will. But I do request the youth that till the time the majority of Indians are living in safer, better conditions, till they are in a position to judge their duties and actions, they should not participate in any kind of revolutionary activities. If they are dedicated to serving the nation, they should participate with full commitment in overground mass movements—otherwise their sacrifices will be fruitless. Their work for mass mobilization among the people will prove more beneficial to the country. Given that the conditions are not conducive to revolutionary activities, getting involved in them is a wasted effort. Those for whom you work will be the very people who will pull you down, and you will only end up dying with bitter resentment.

My last appeal to the fellow countrymen is that whatever you choose to do, be united in your efforts and work towards the betterment of the country. This is the only path to everyone's emancipation.

Marte 'Bismil', 'Roshan', 'Lahiri', 'Ashfaq' atyachaar se
Honge paida sainkadon veer inke rudhir ki dhaar se.

Bismil, Roshan, Lahiri, Ashfaq die at the
hands of tyranny.
Hundreds of brave souls shall be born from
their blood.

Scan QR code to access the
Penguin Random House India website